Copyright 2021 Neander Books©
All rights reserved.

All rights reserved. No part of this book may be reproduced, stored in a retrieval system or transmitted, in amy form or by any means, electronic, mechanical, photocopying or otherwise without the permission of the publisher.

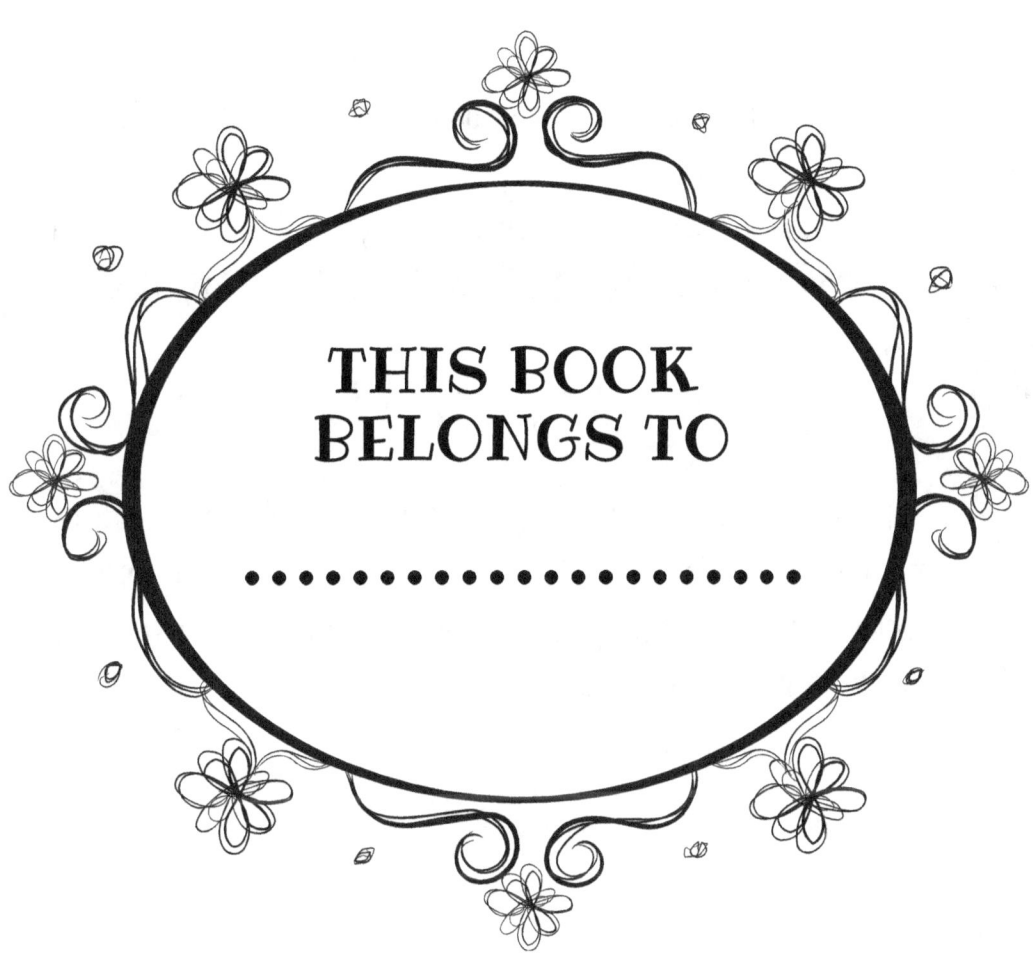

THIS BOOK BELONGS TO

....

INSTRUCTIONS

 Turn off the distractions around you and relax.

 Have fun! There is no wrong way to color, and with this book you are is sure to have hours of relaxation and enjoyment.

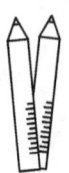 This book works best with color pencils or markers. Wet mediums might bleed through. As images are printed one side only, you may place a piece of paper or card if you notice bleed through.

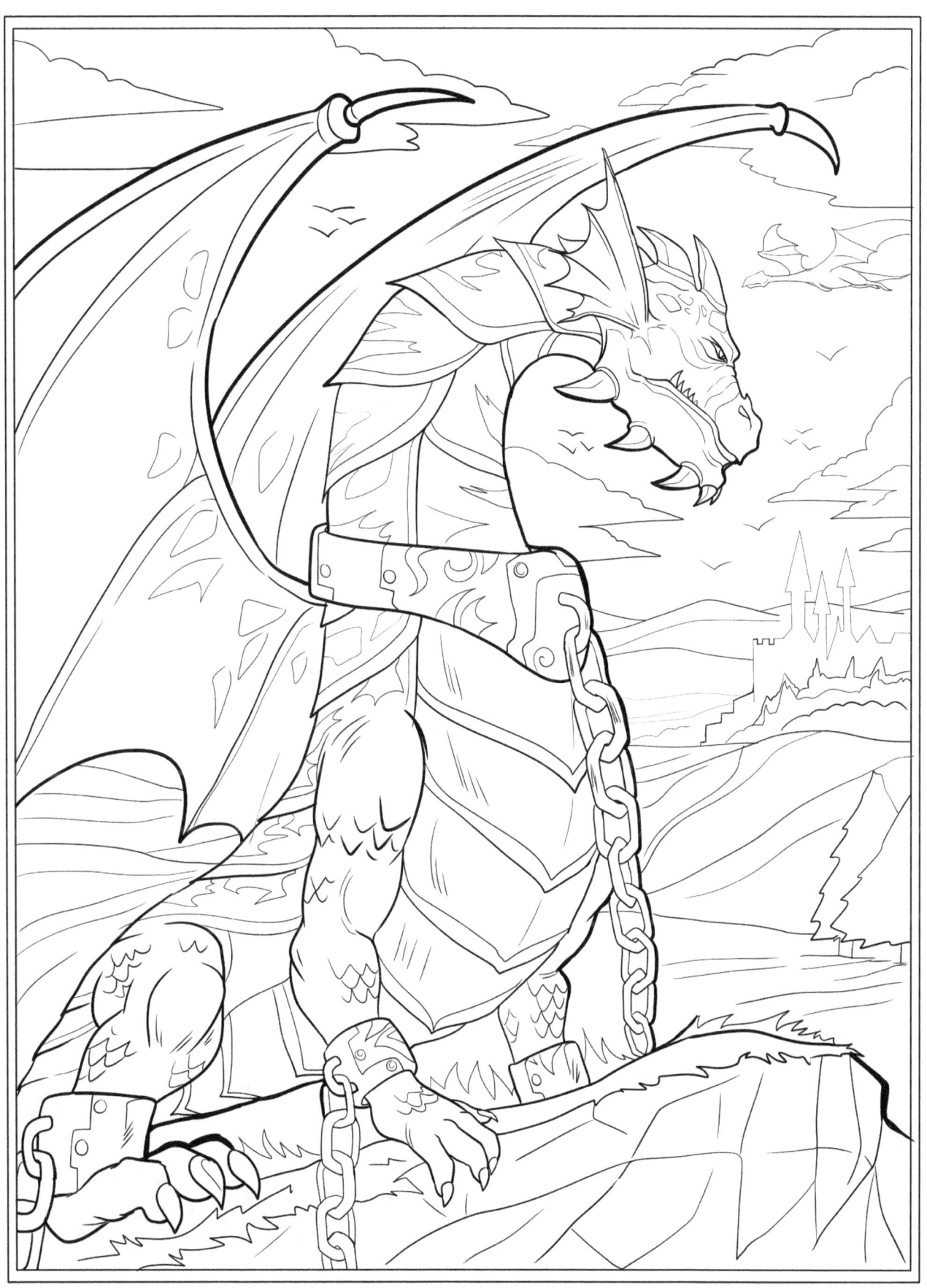

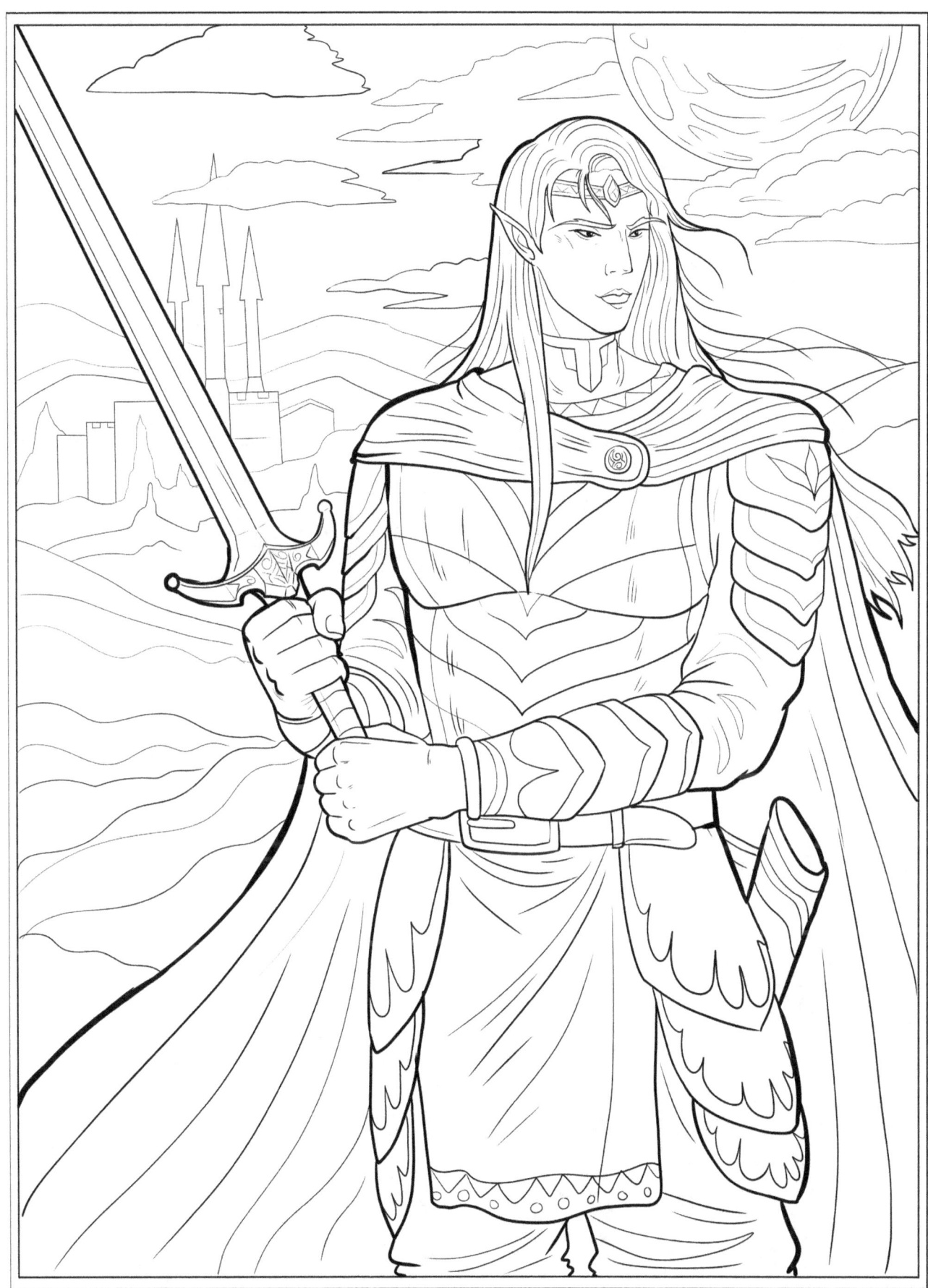

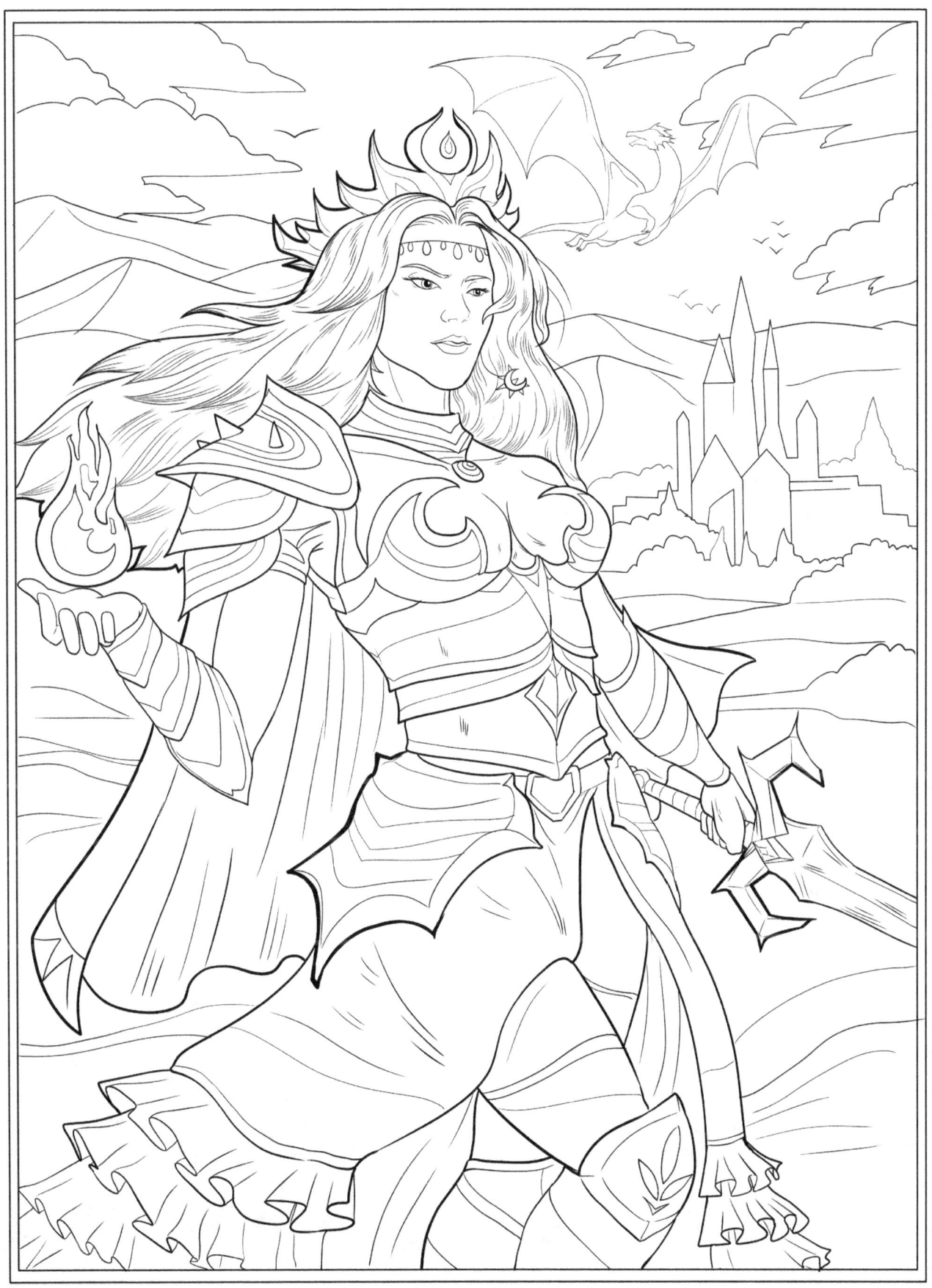

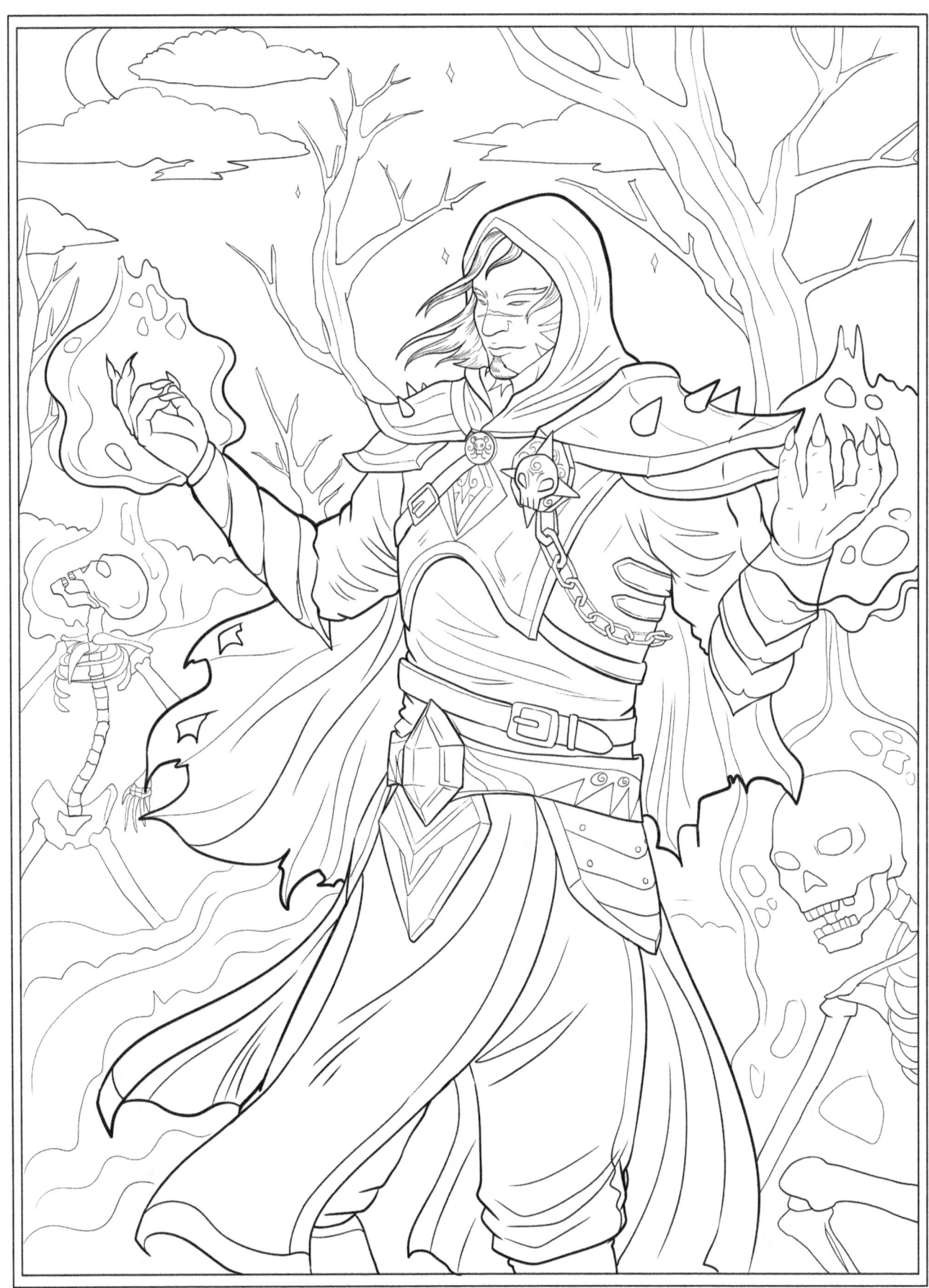

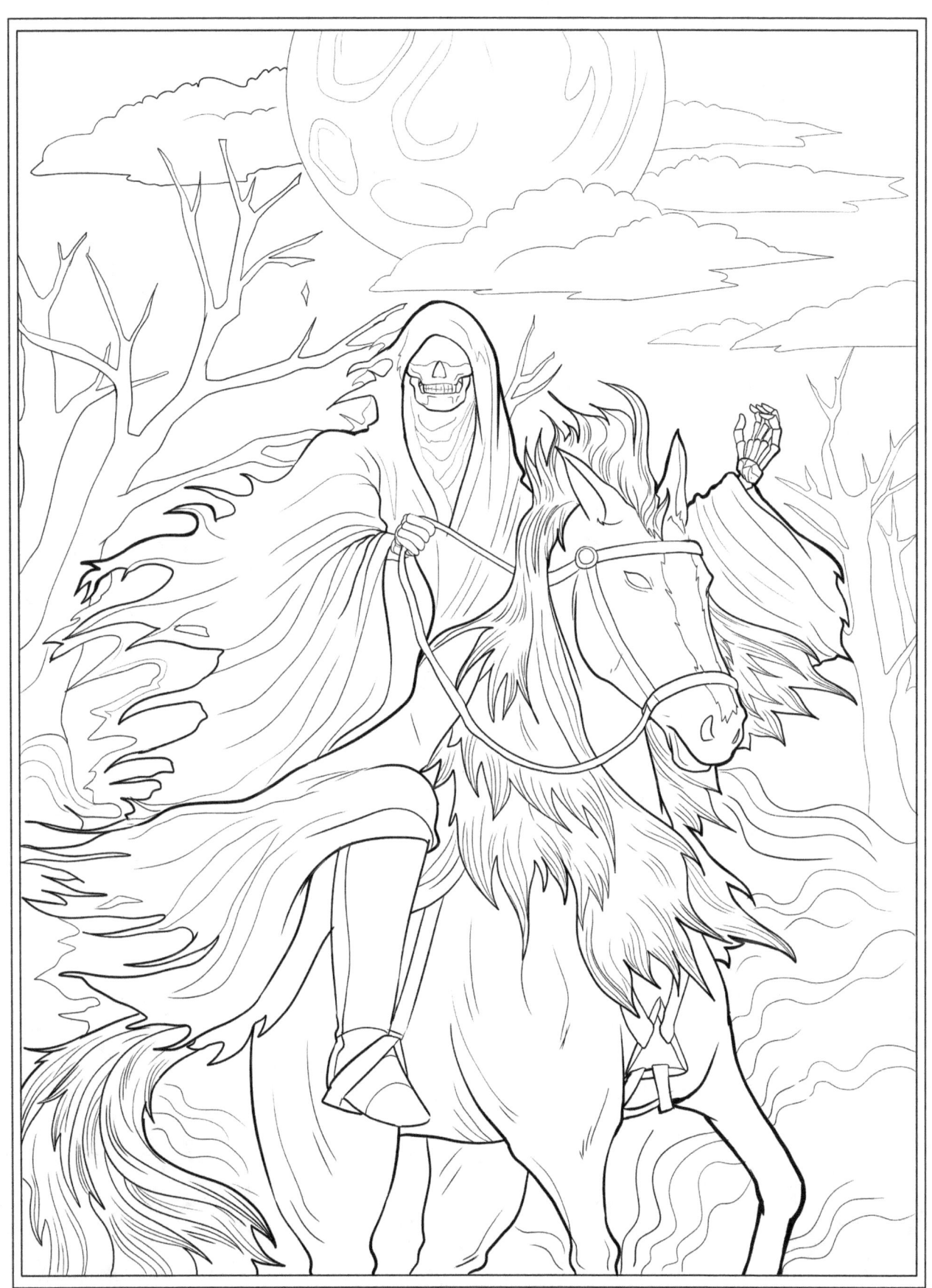

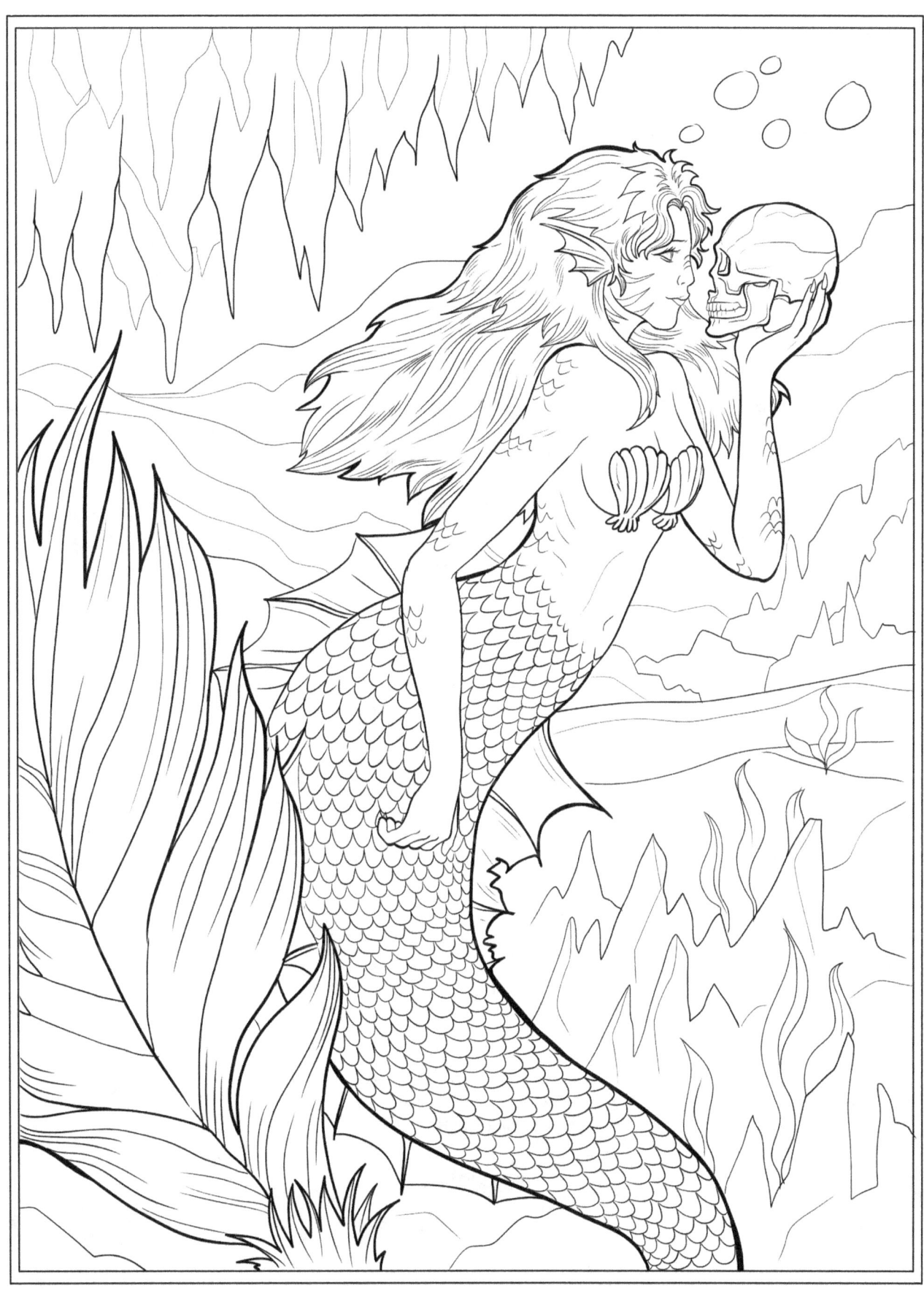

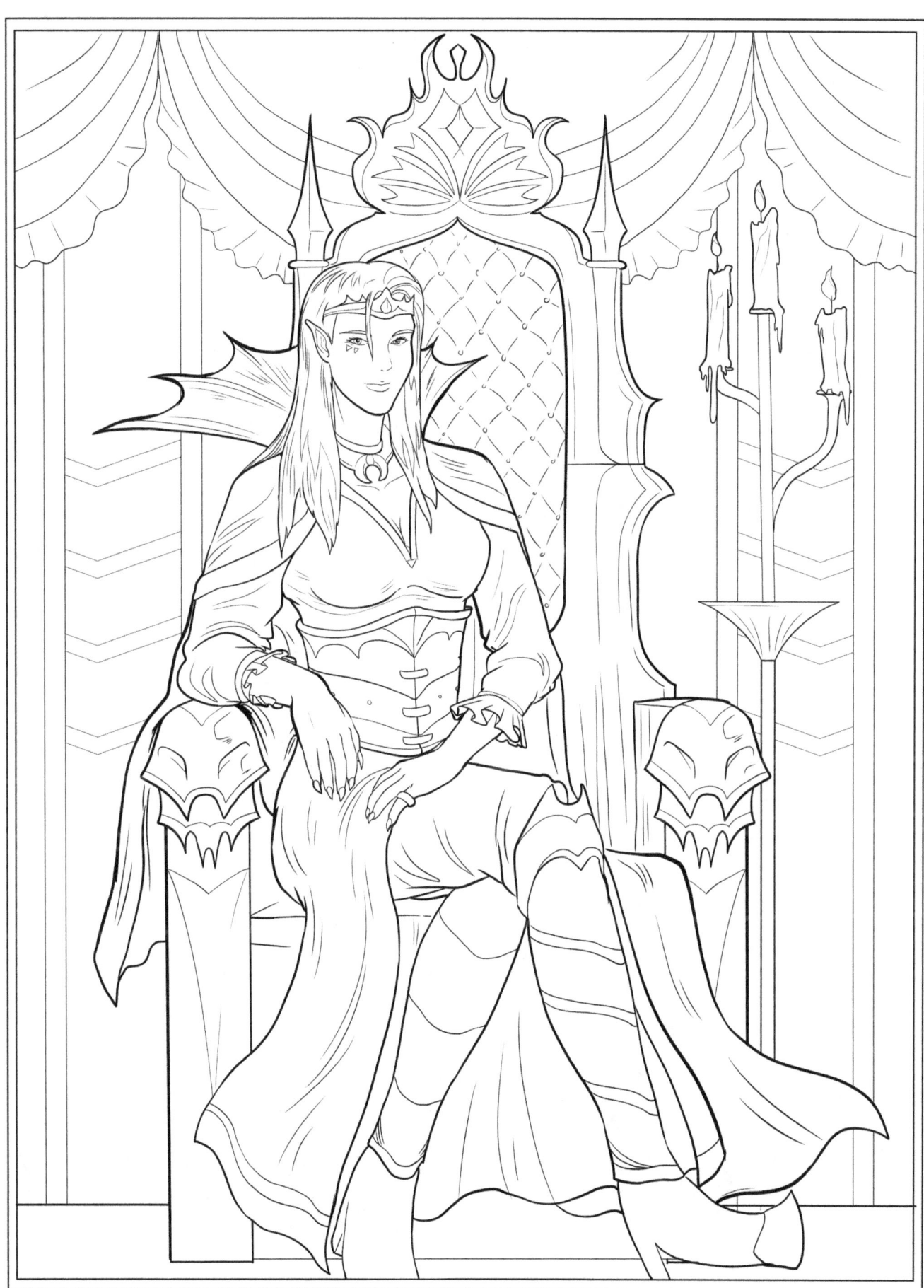

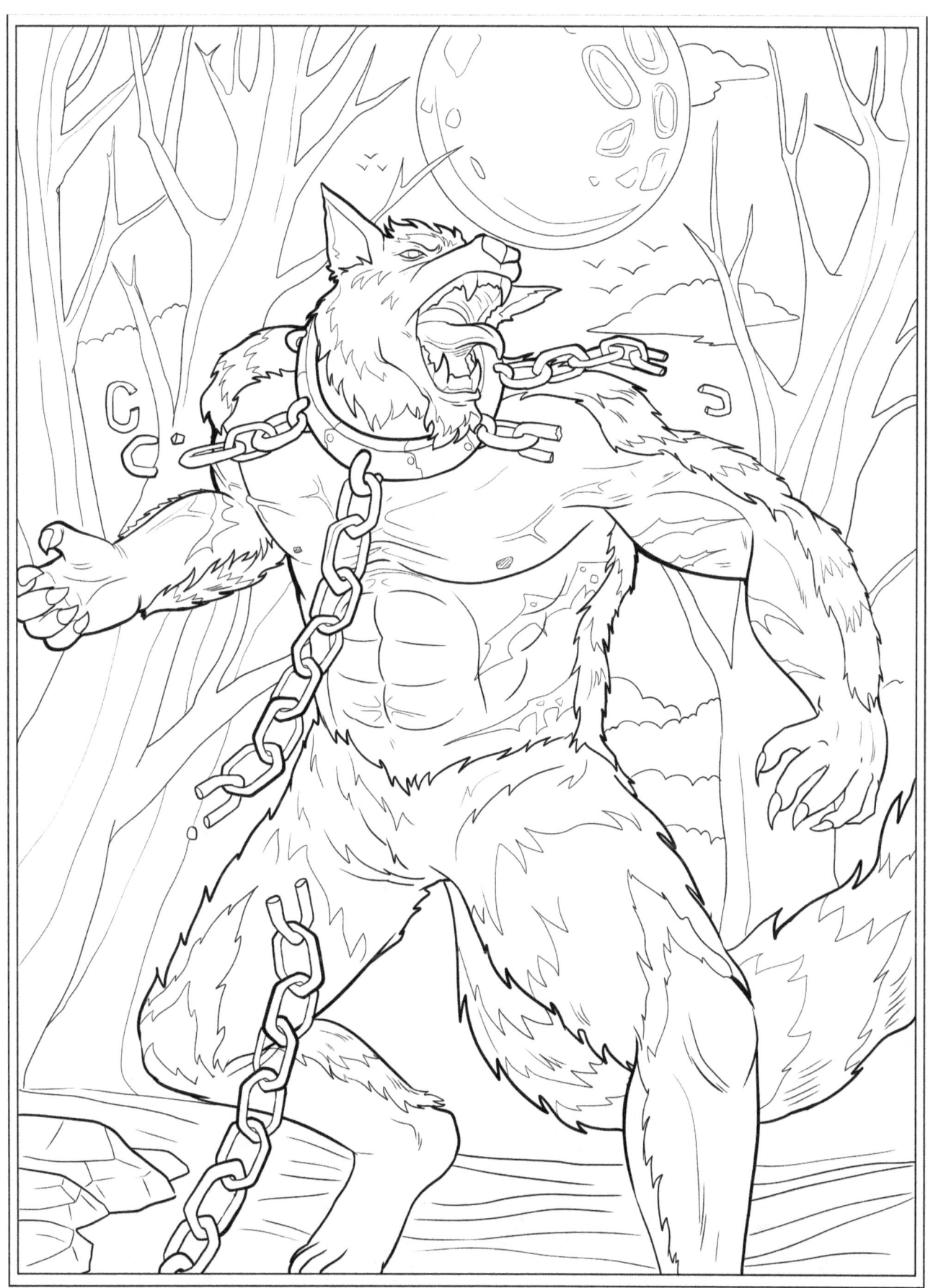

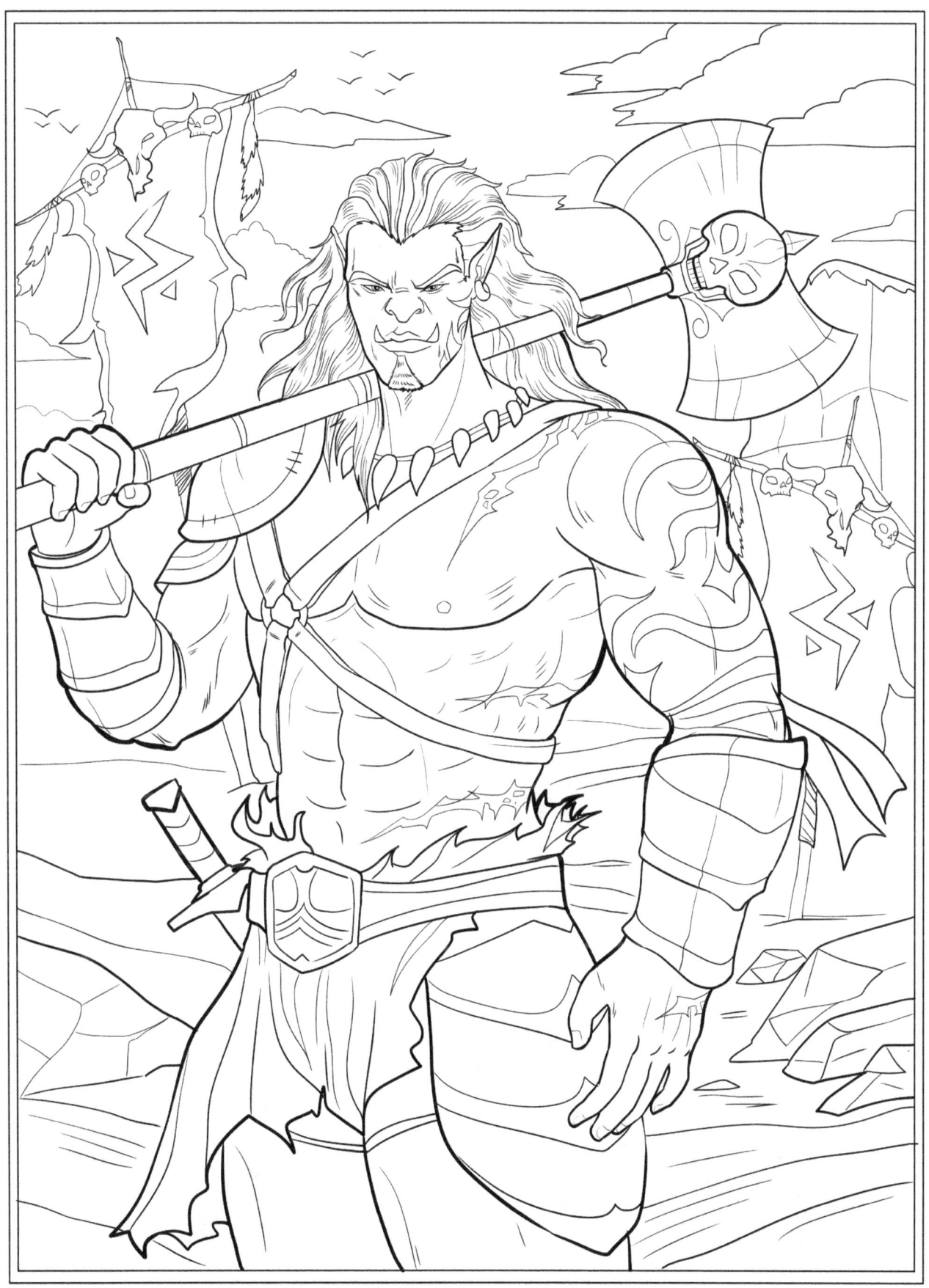

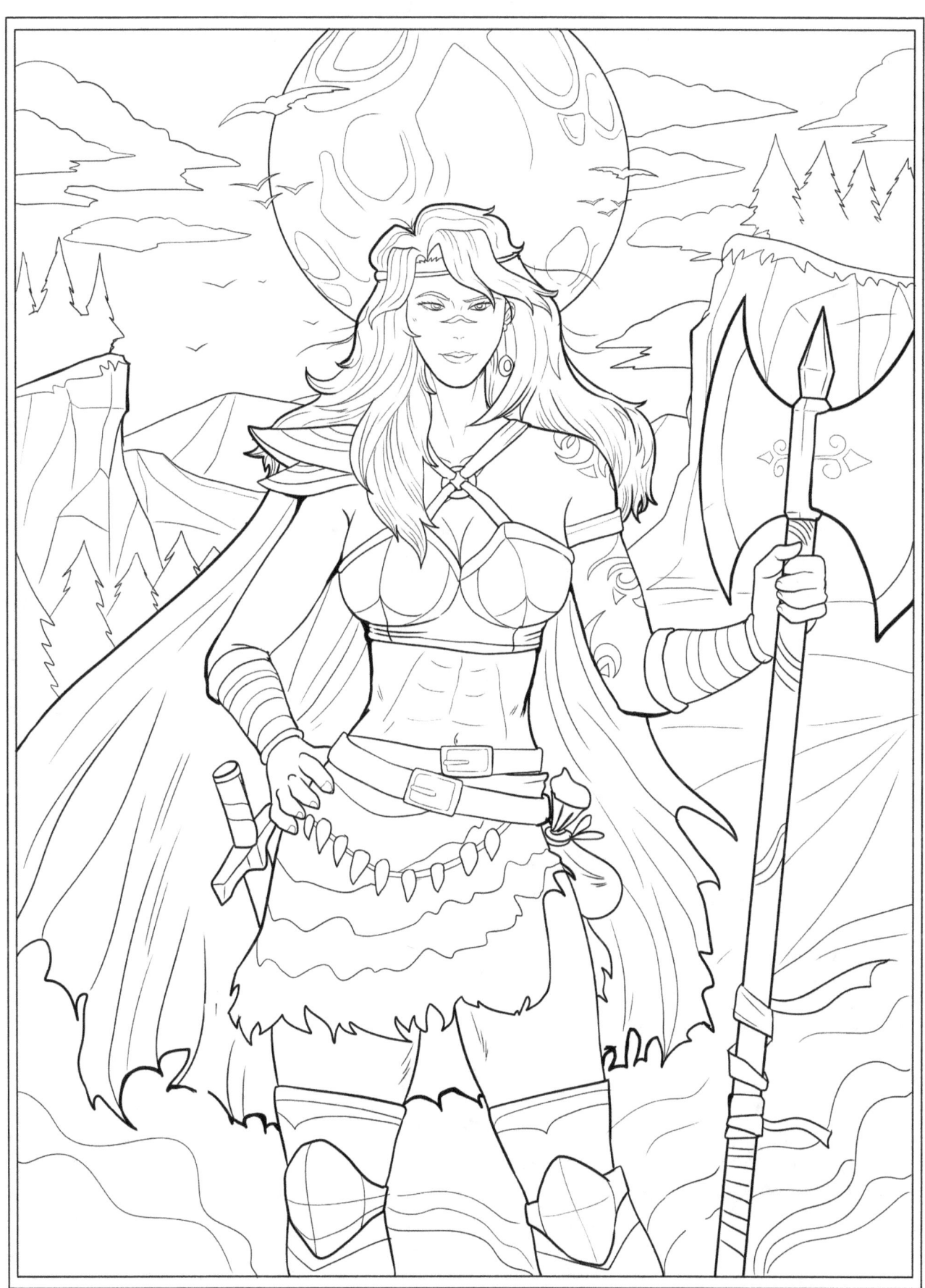

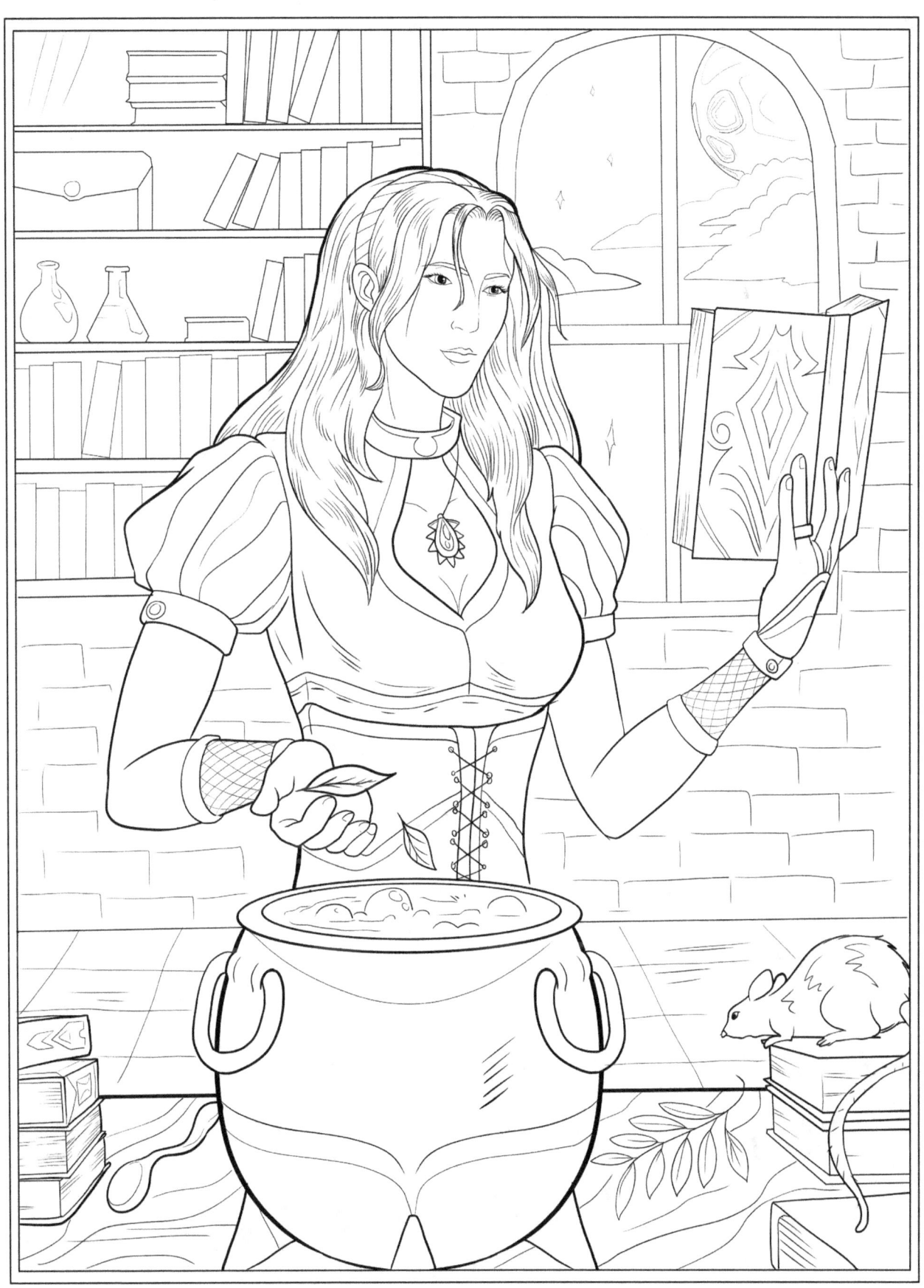

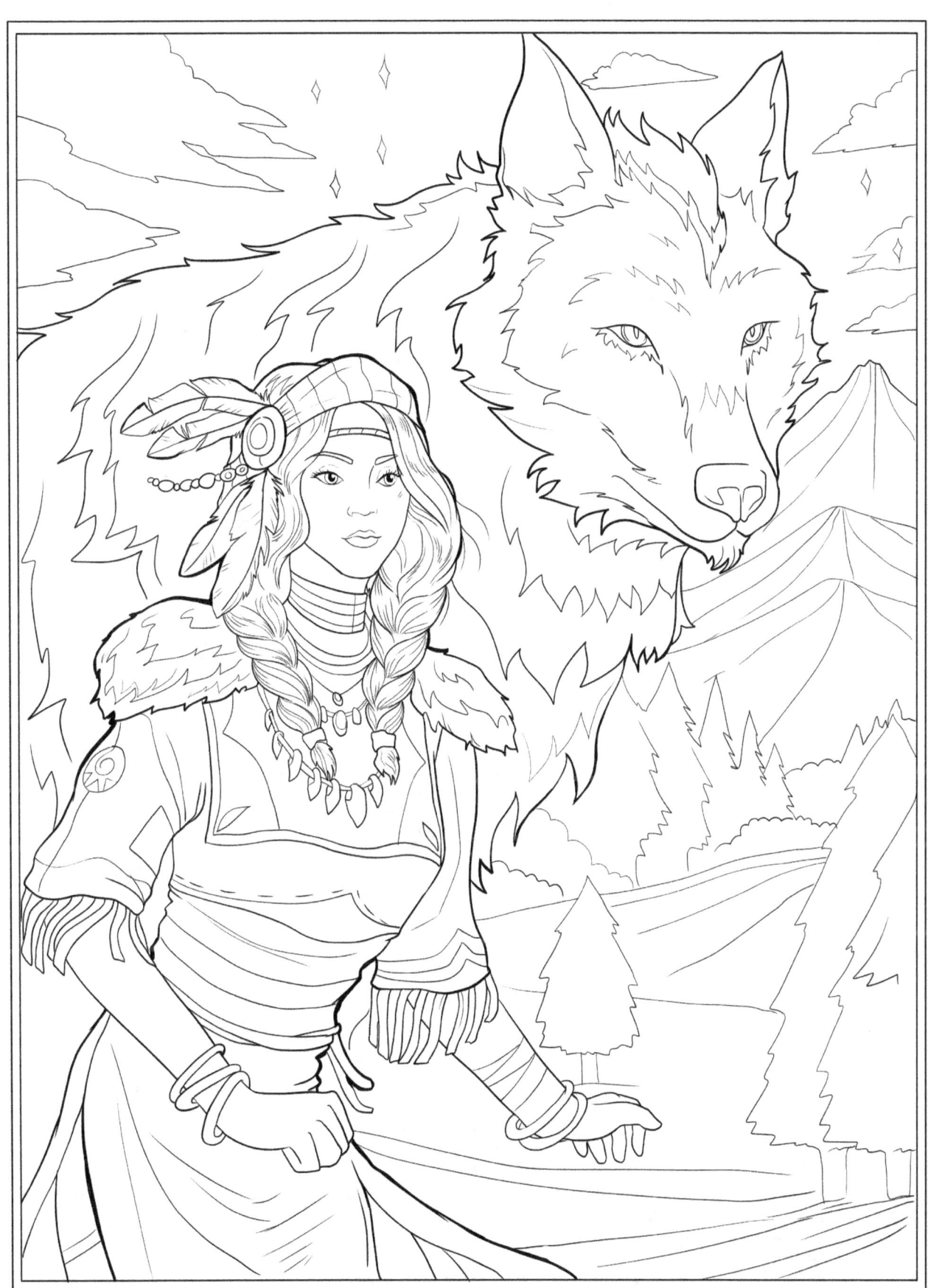

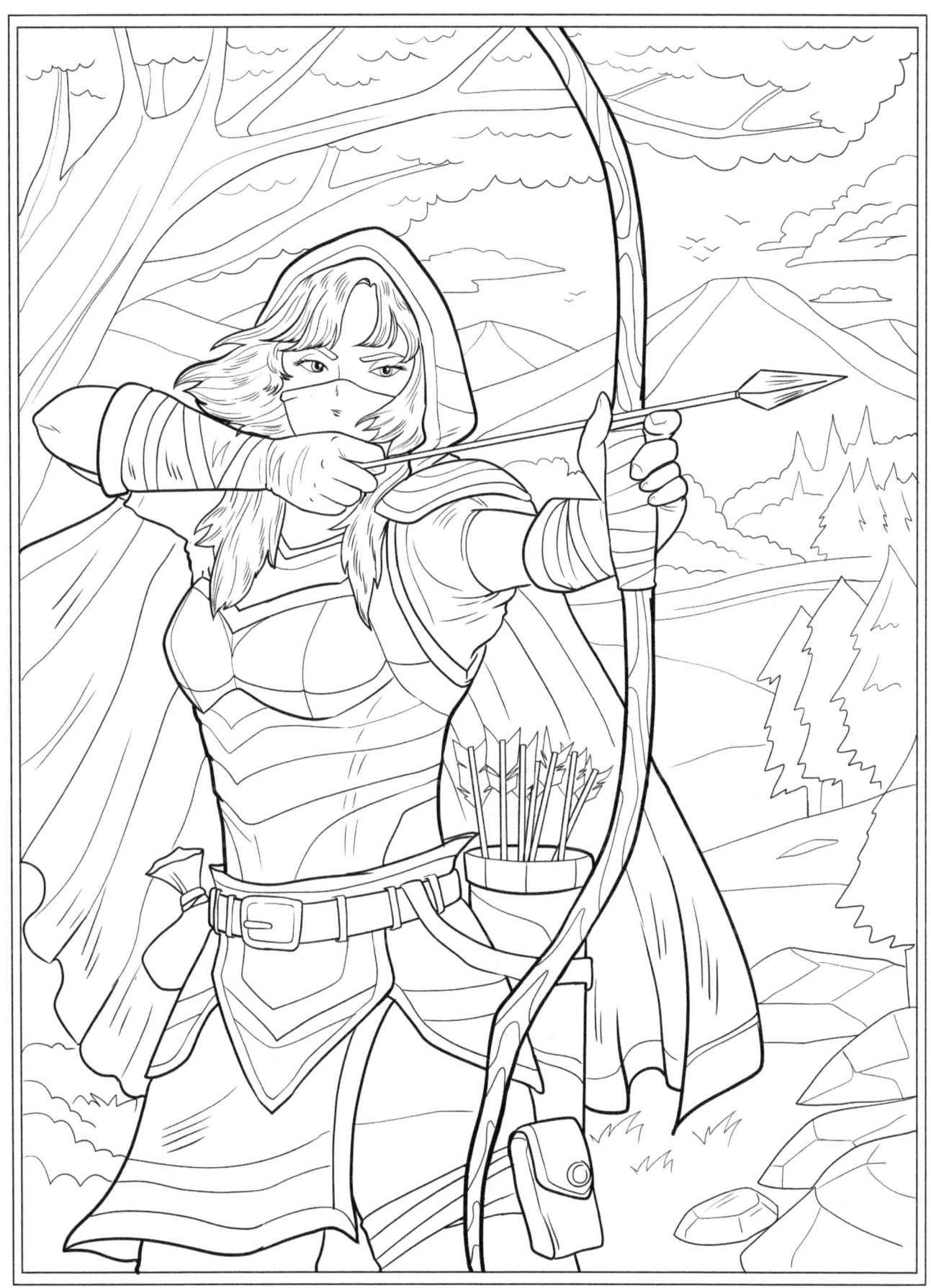

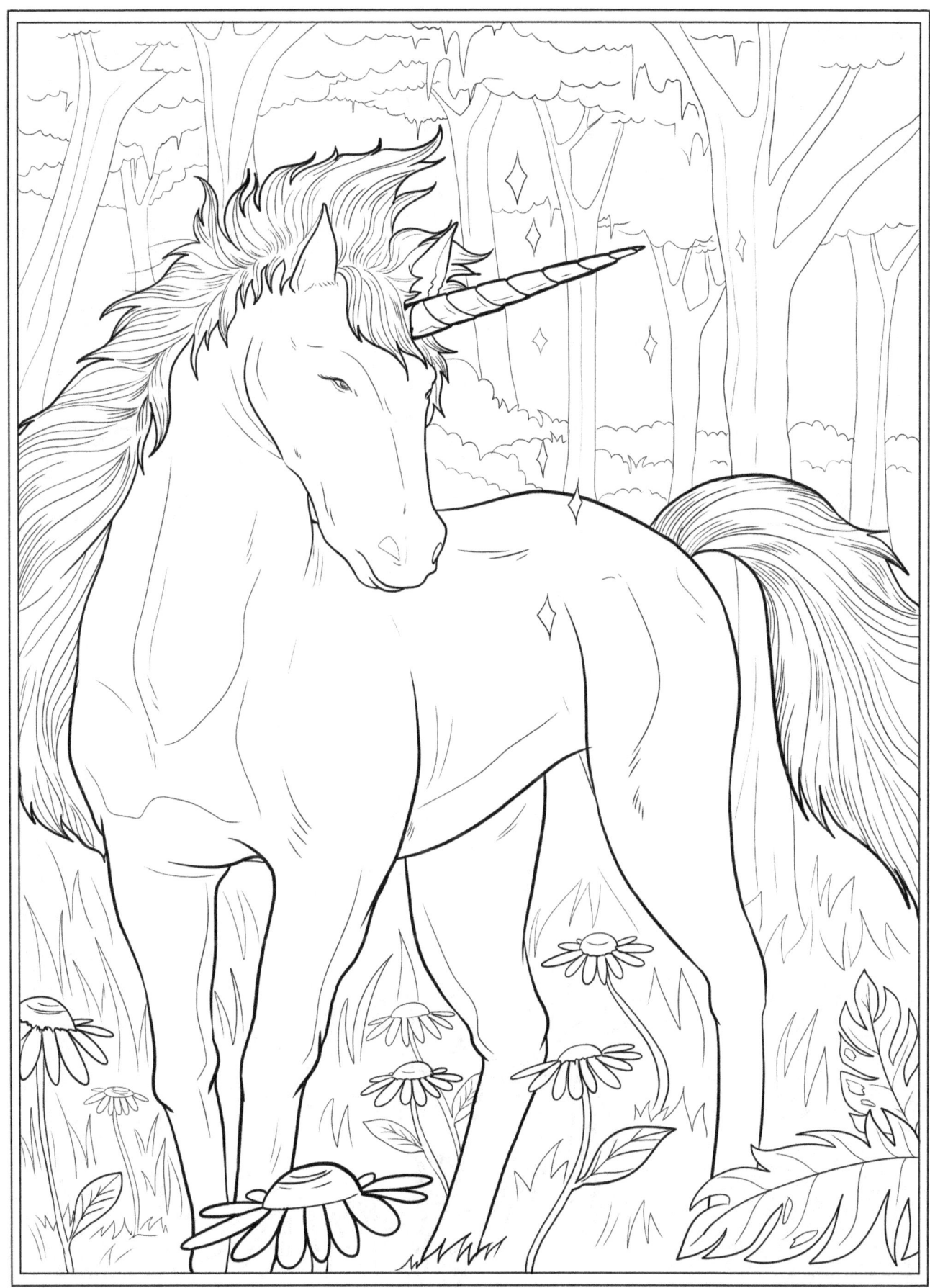

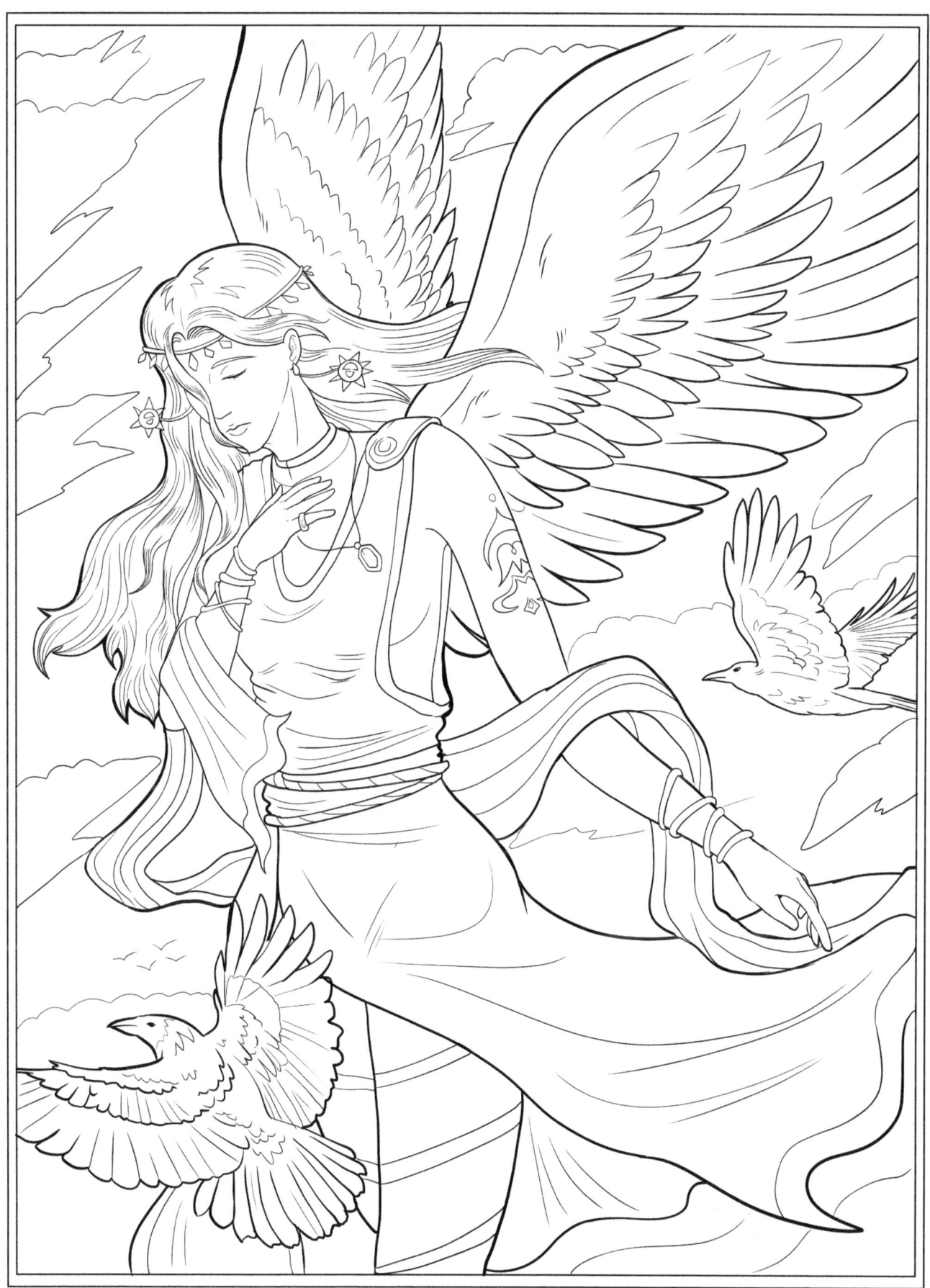

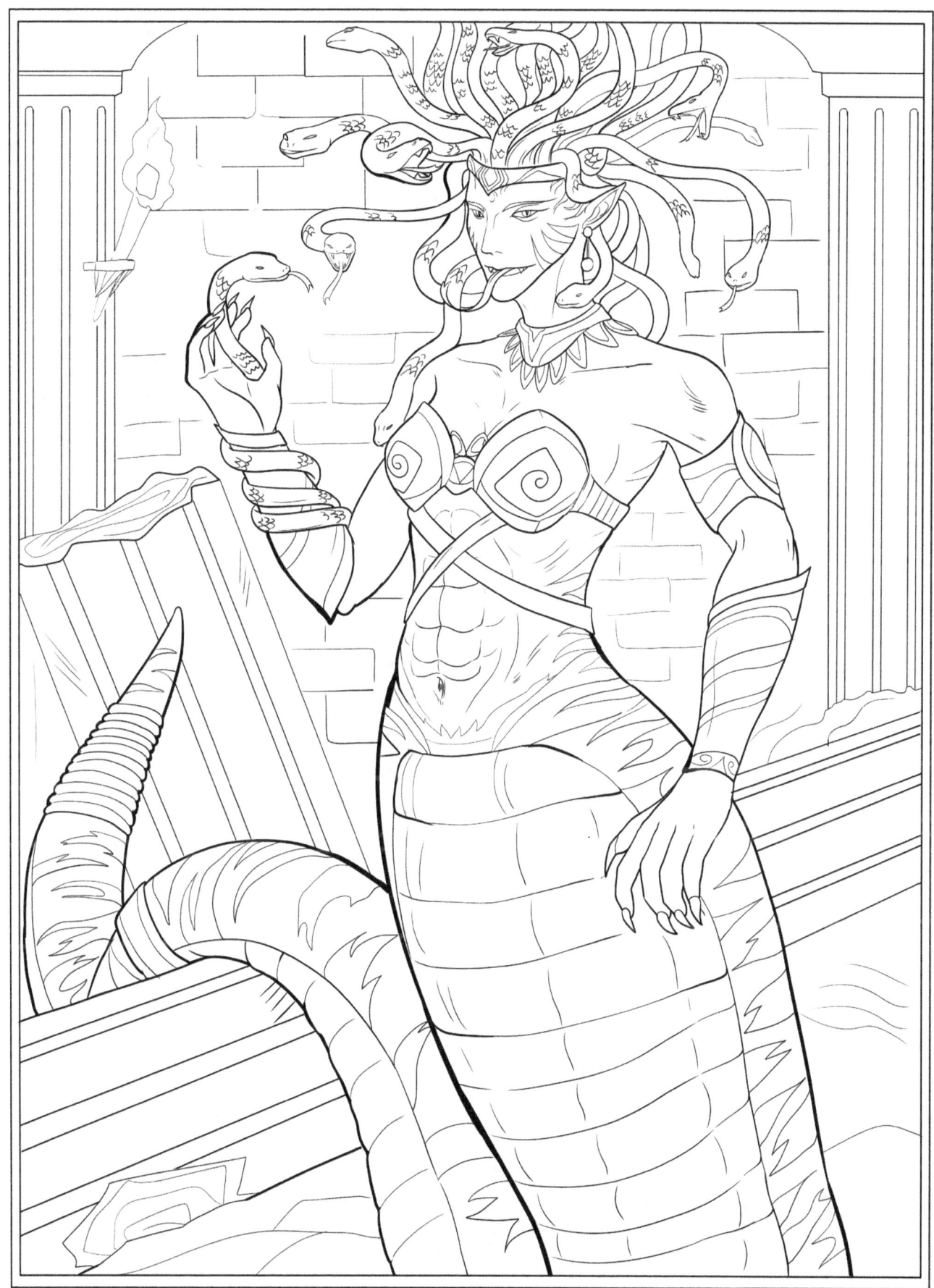

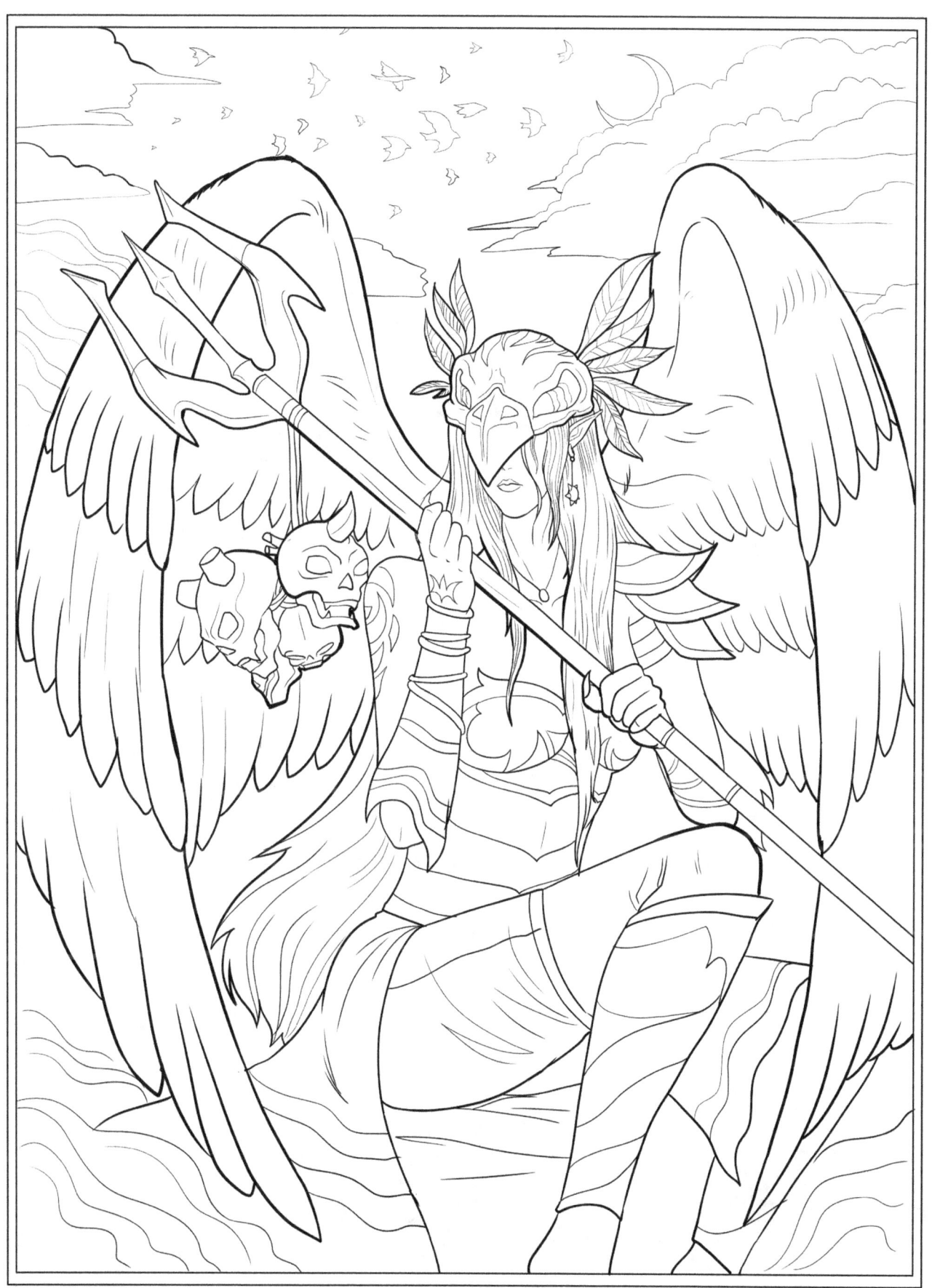

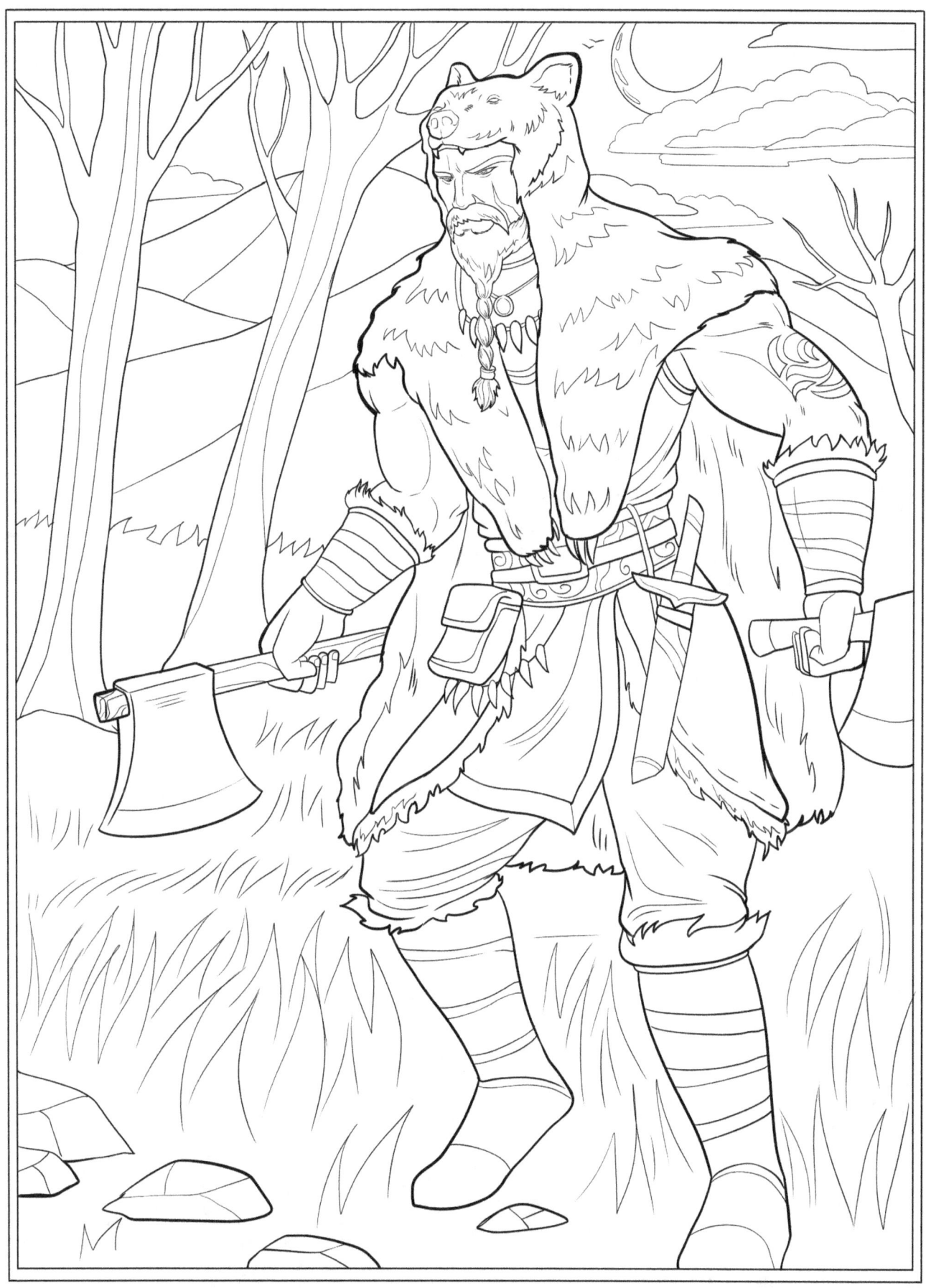

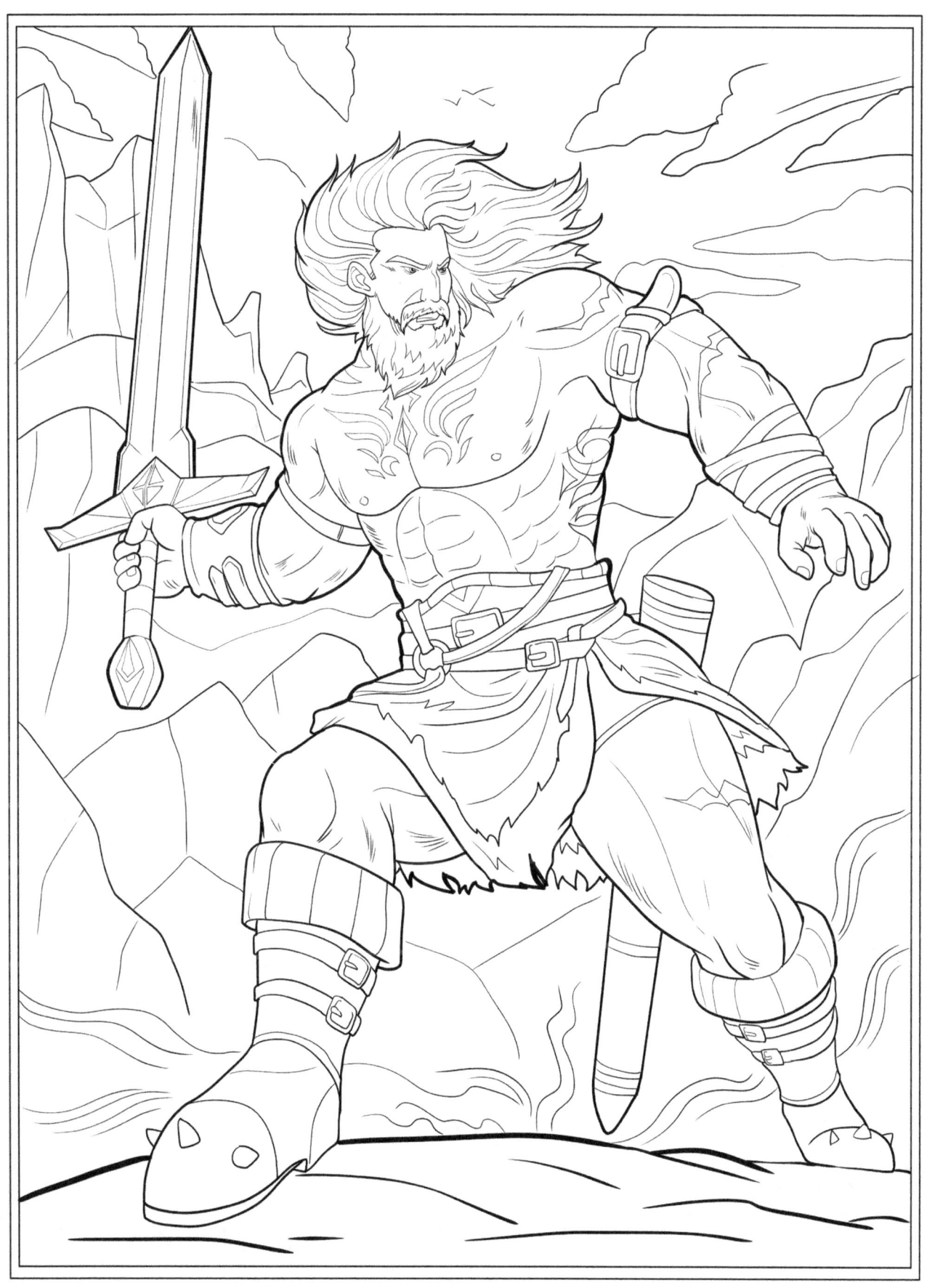

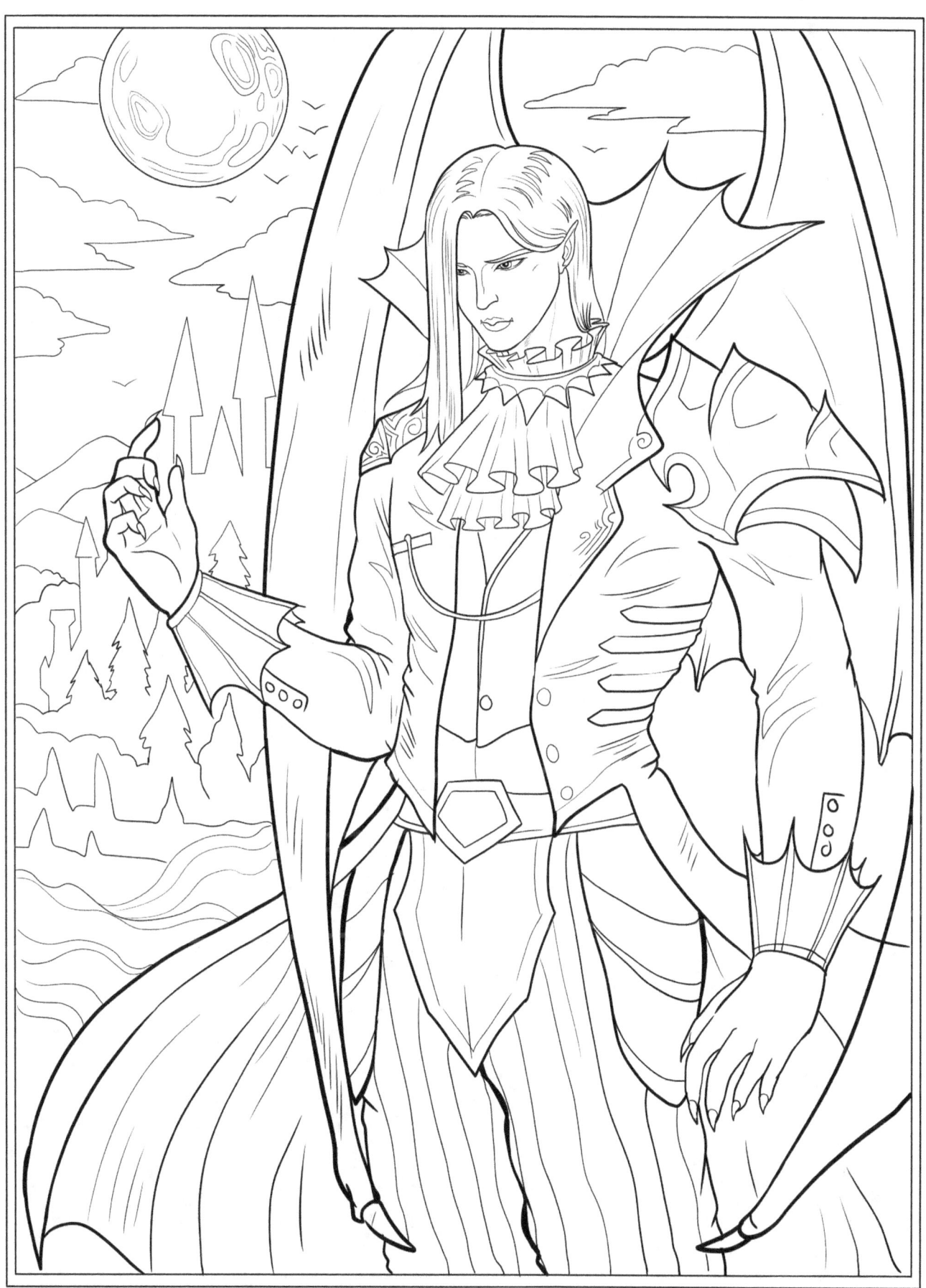

Second set of pages

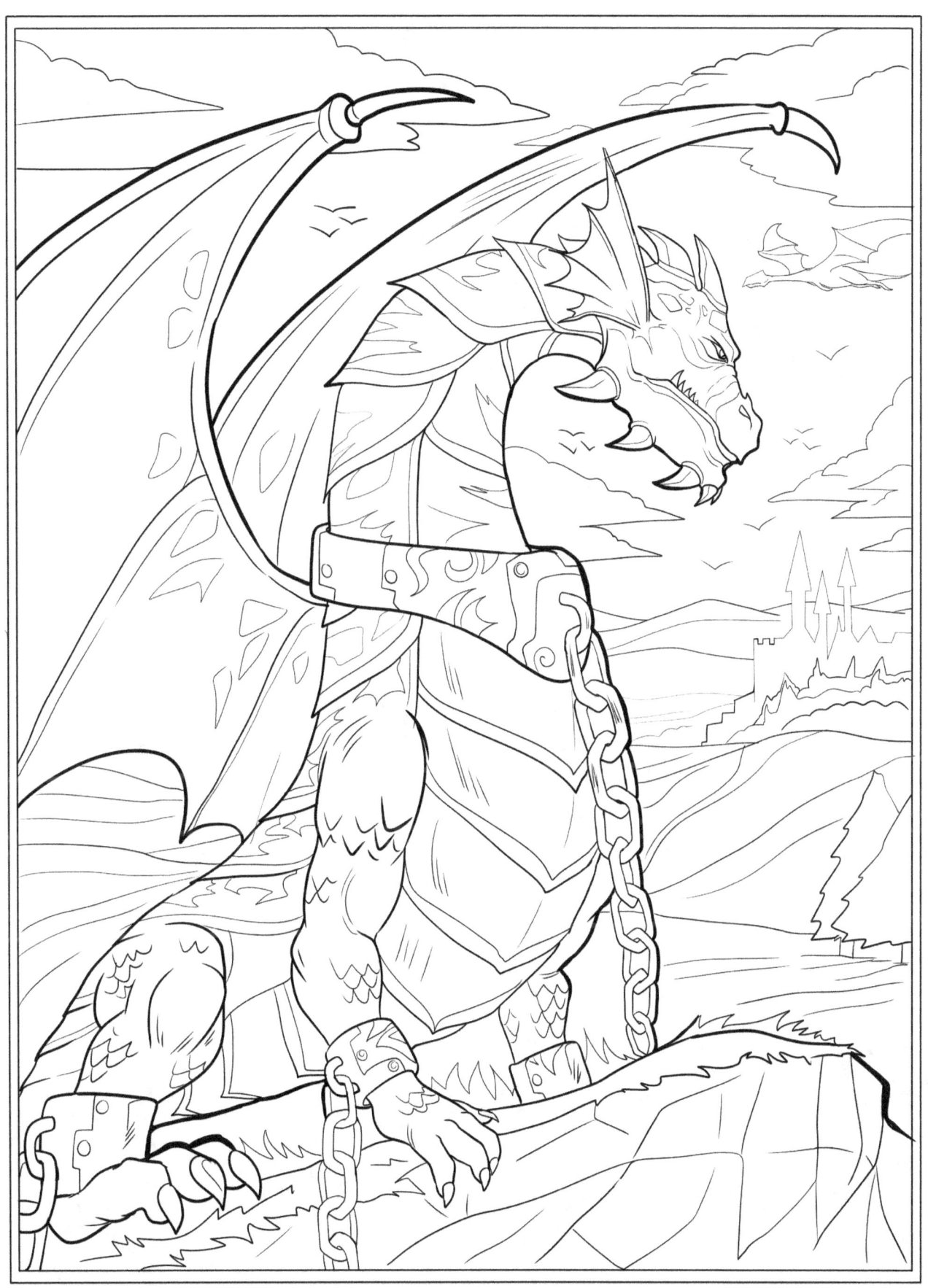

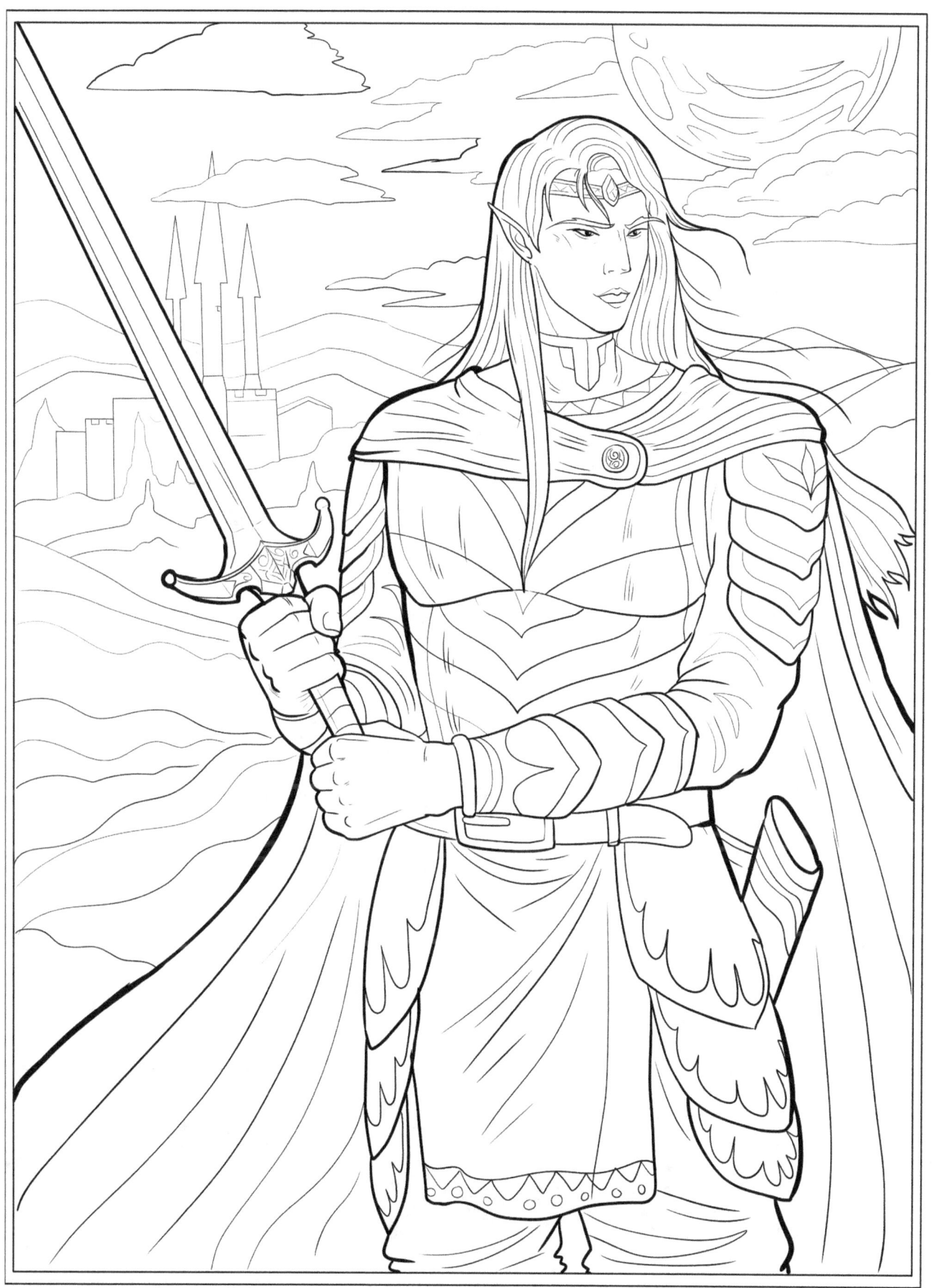

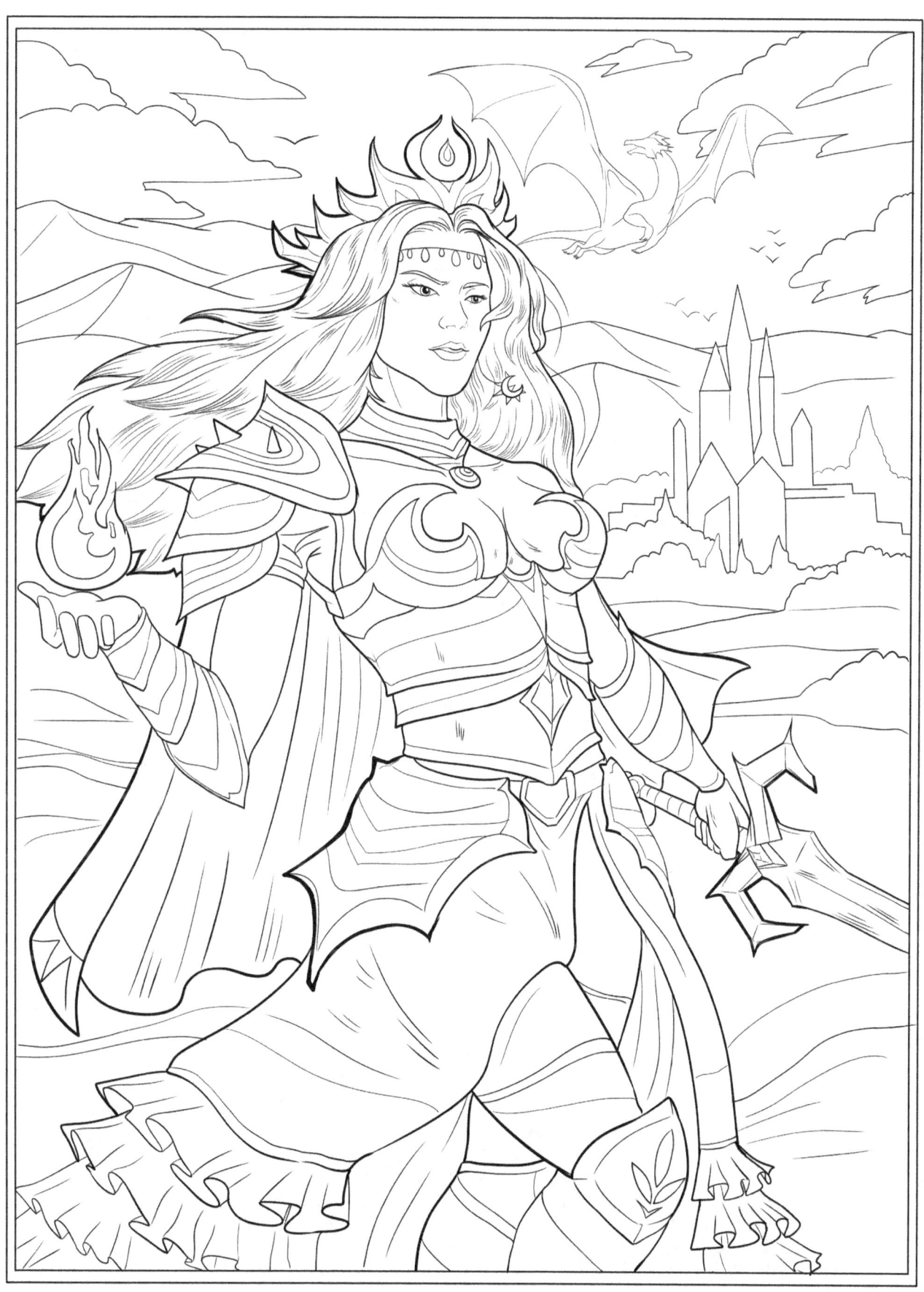

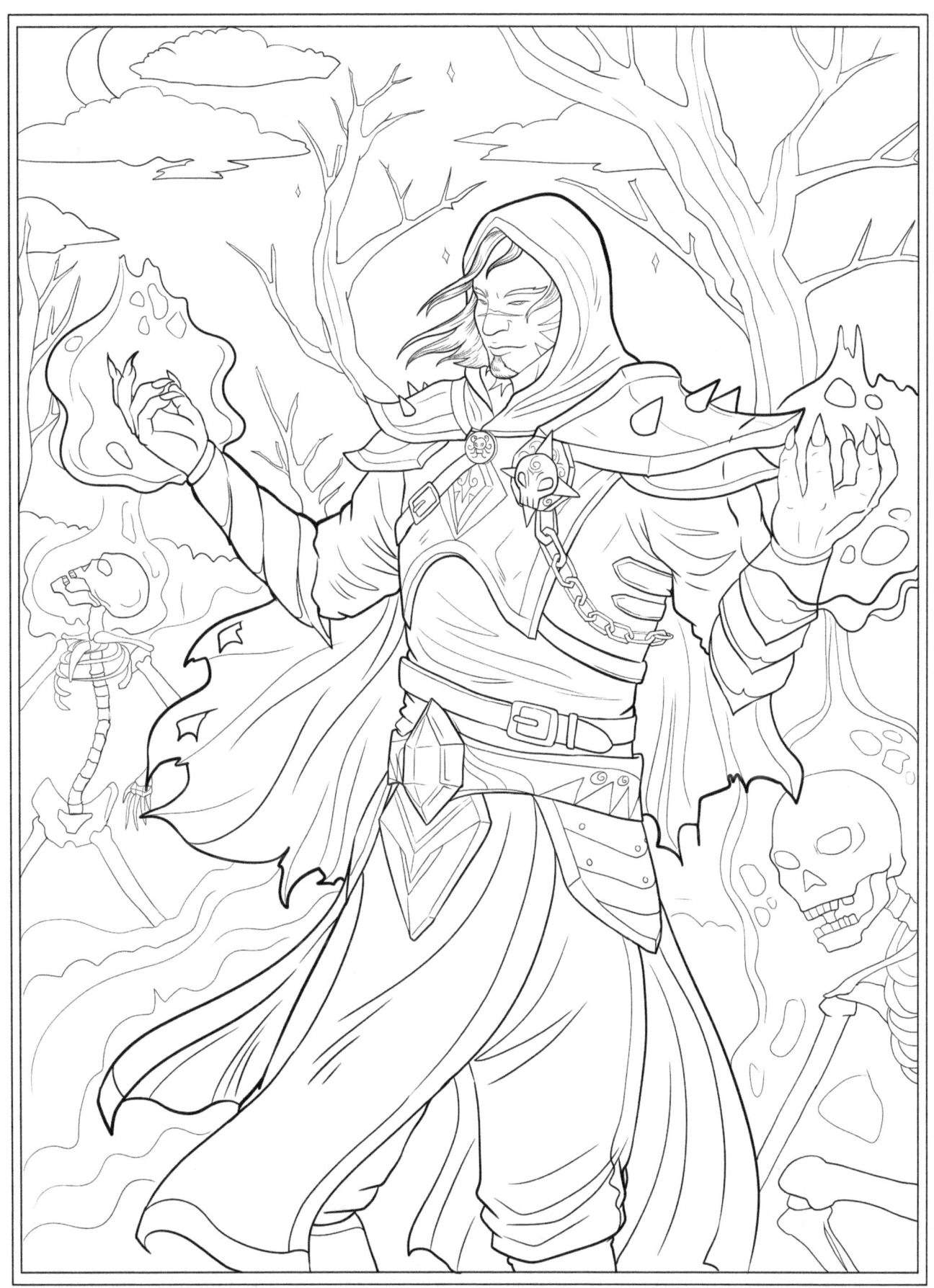

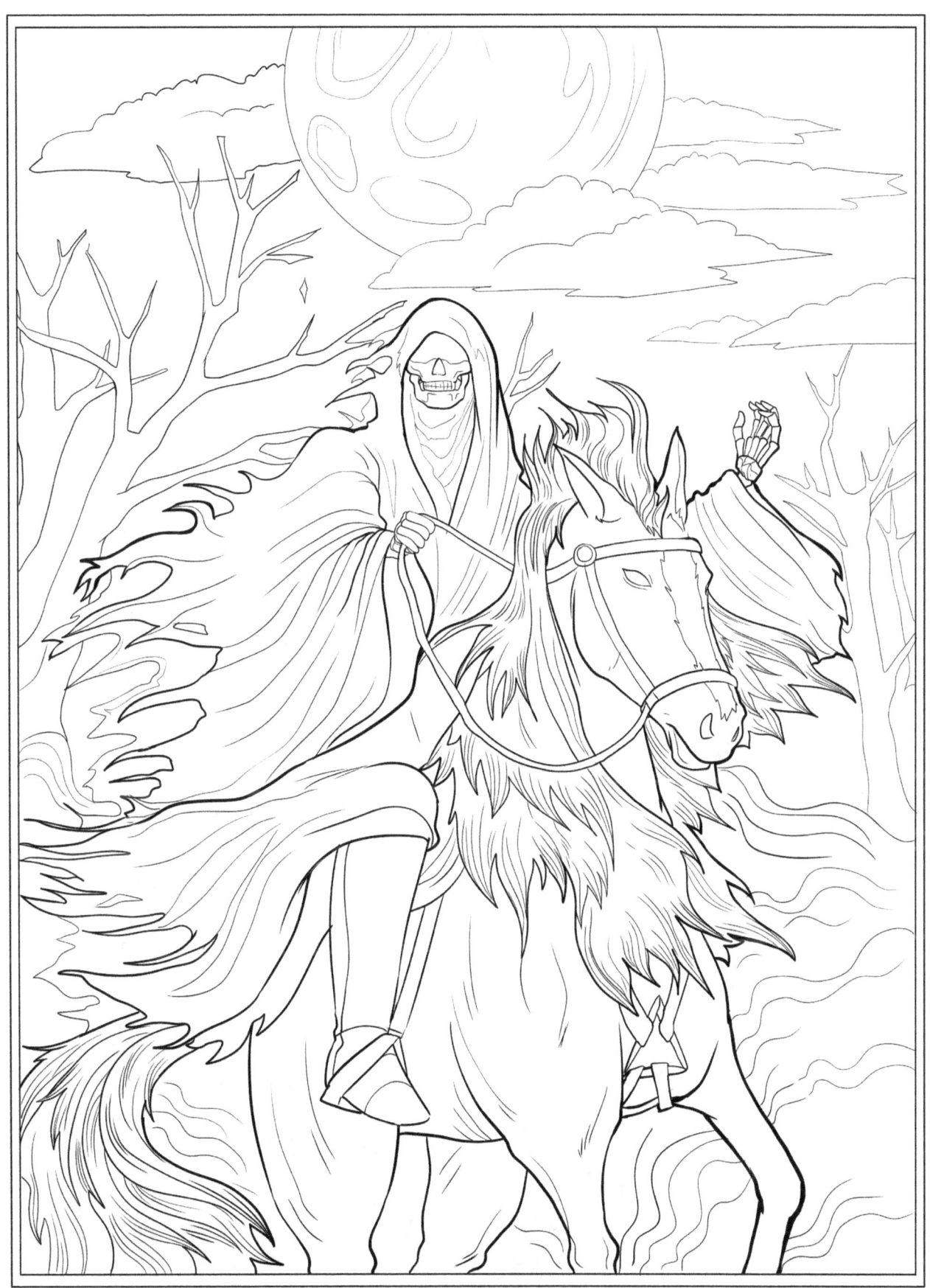

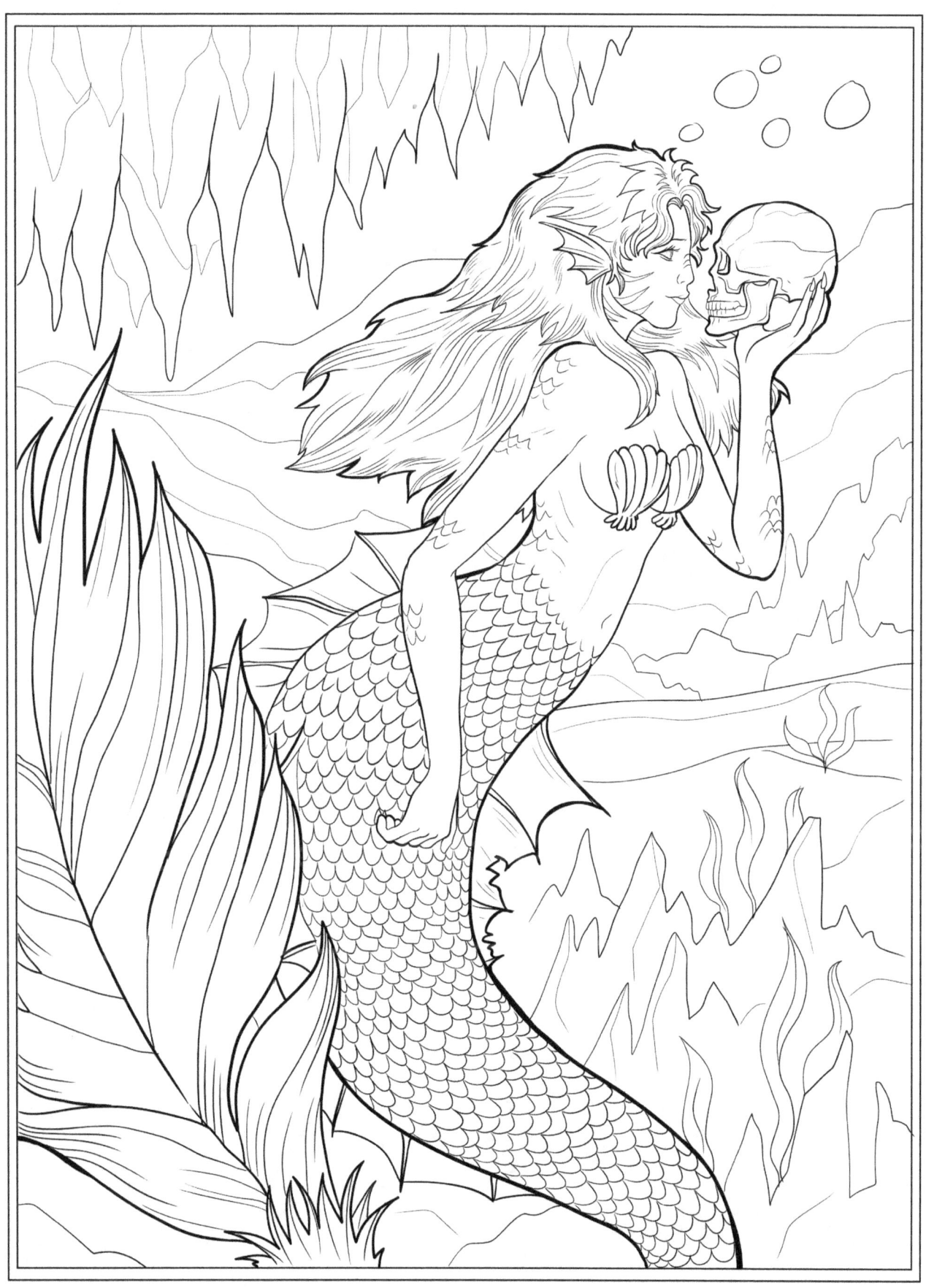

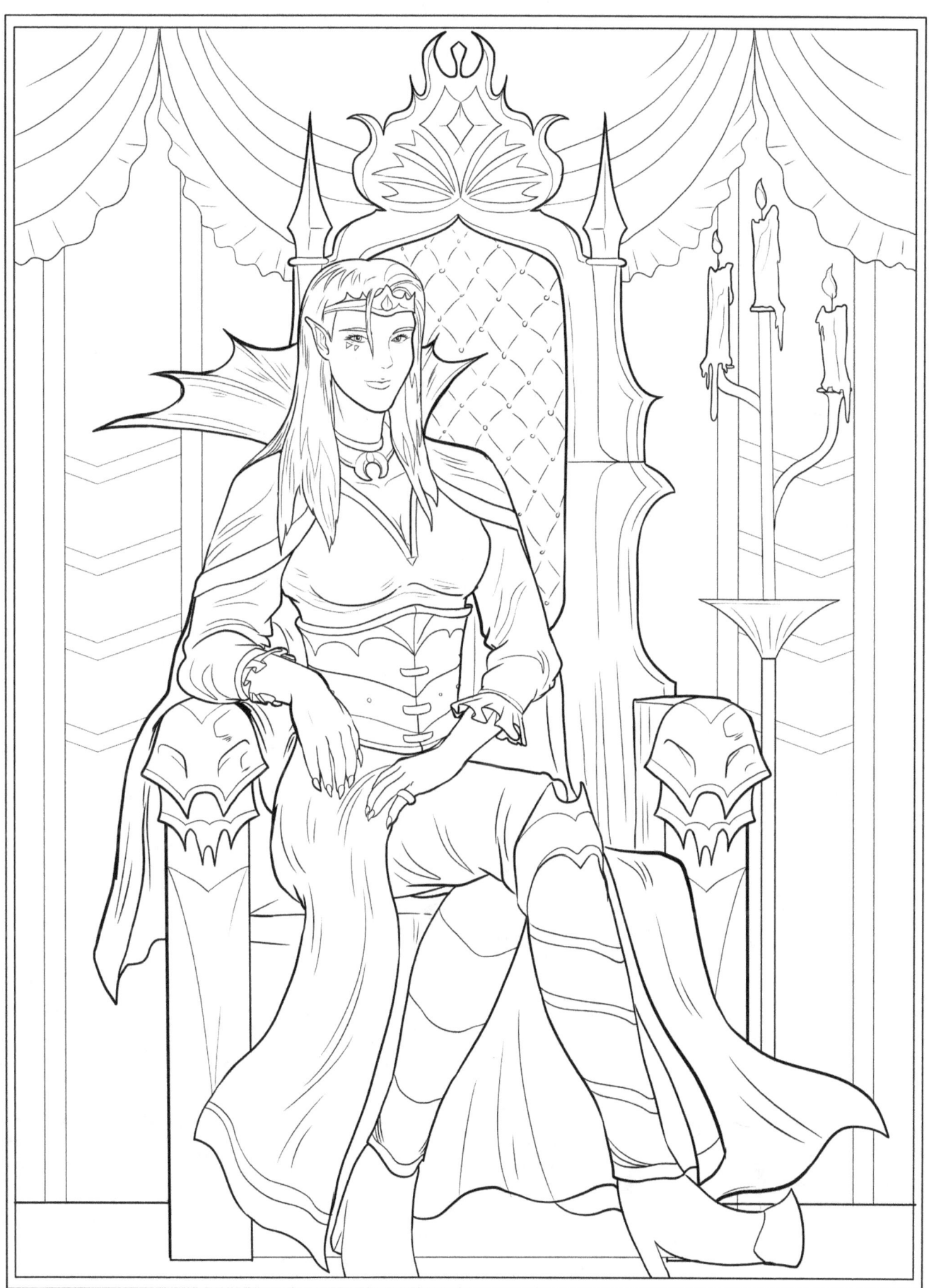

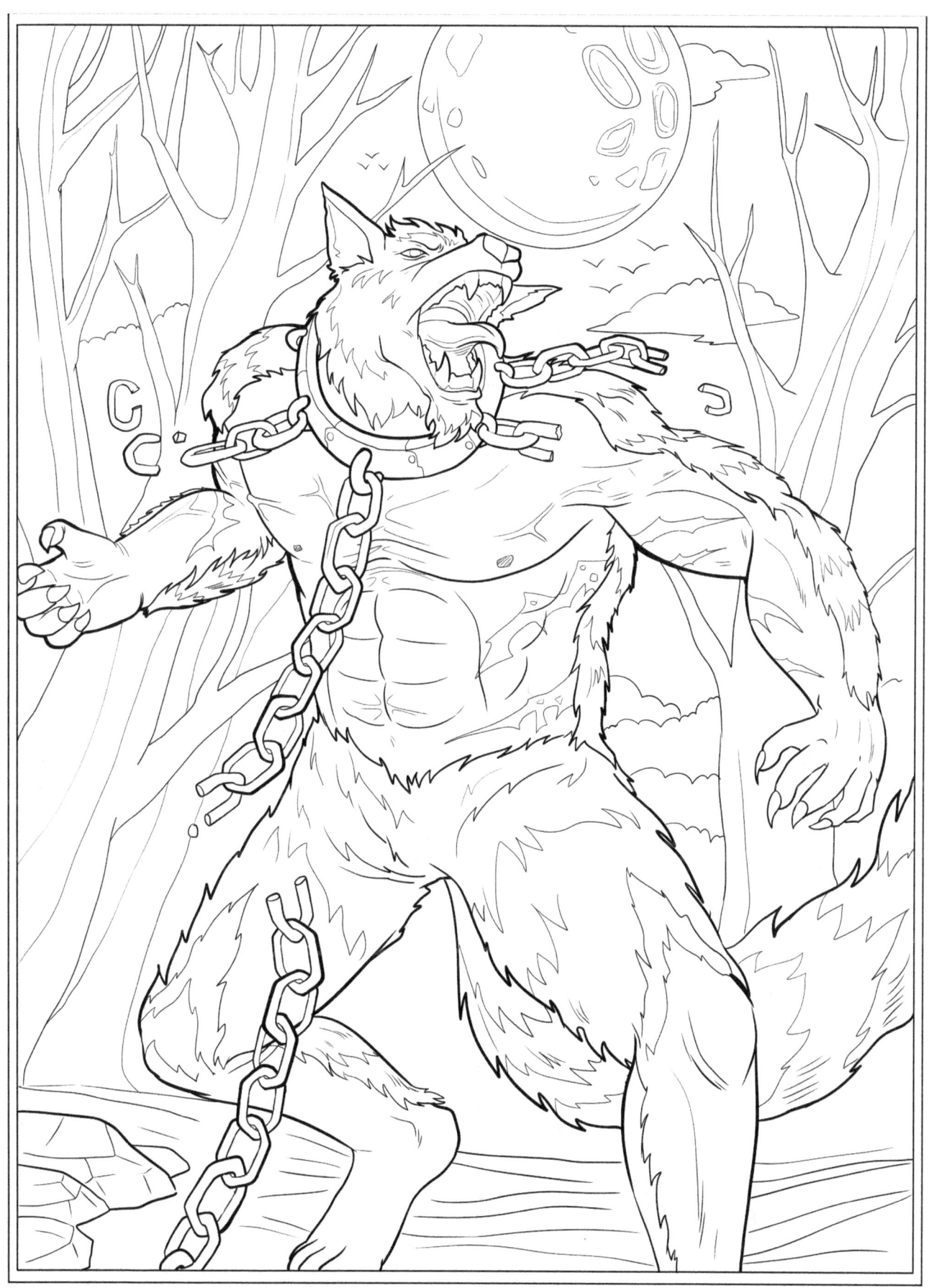

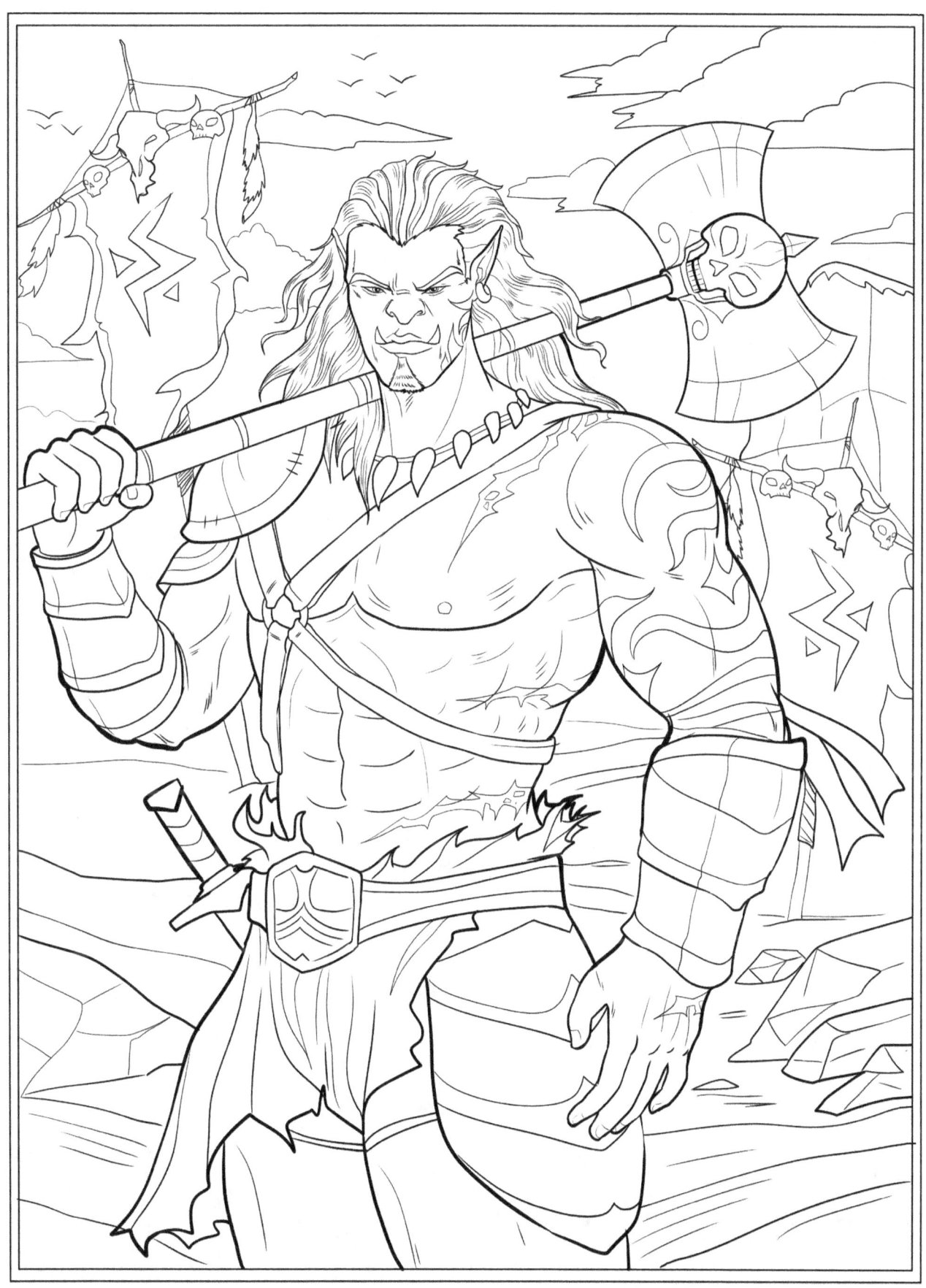

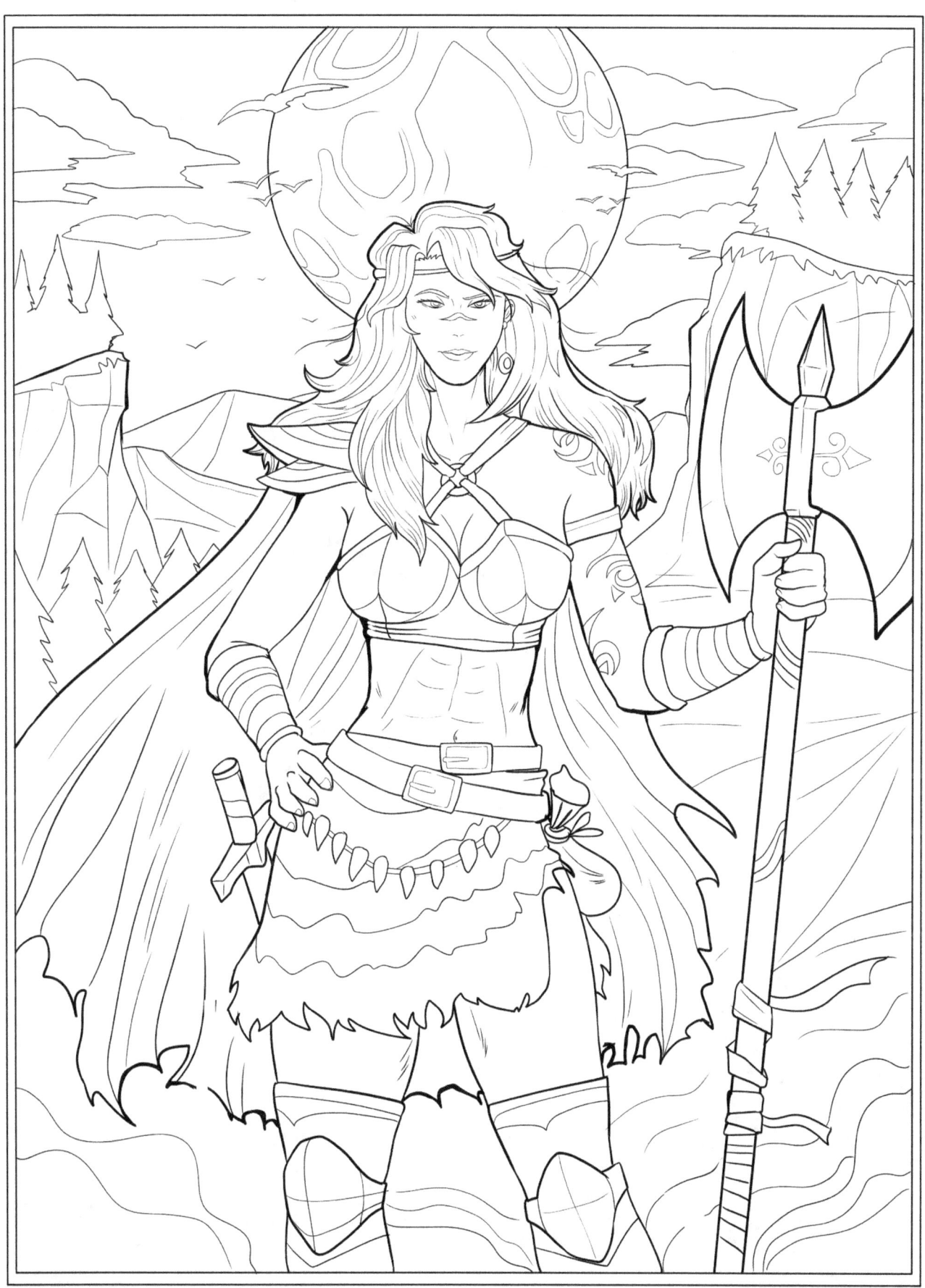

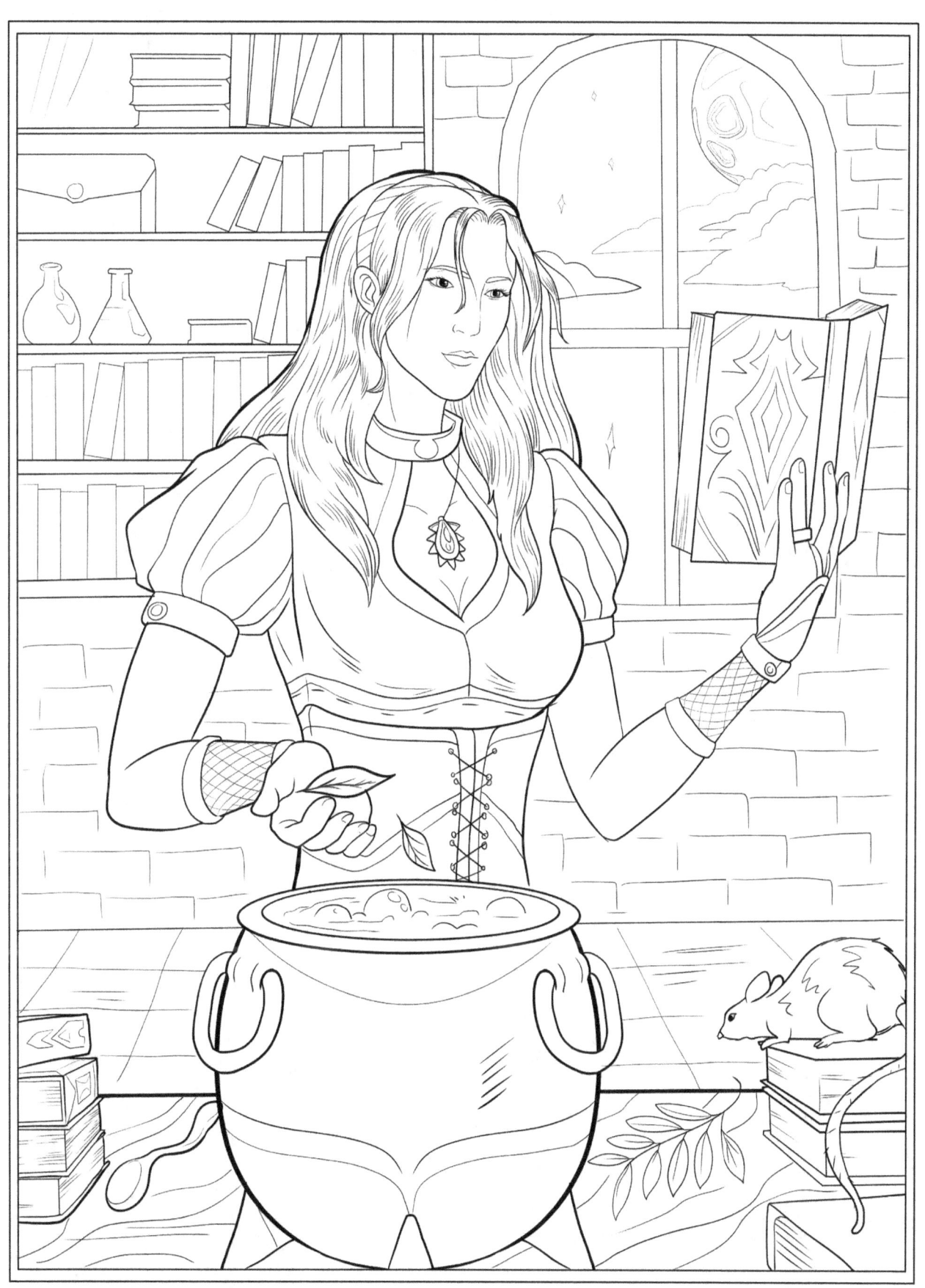

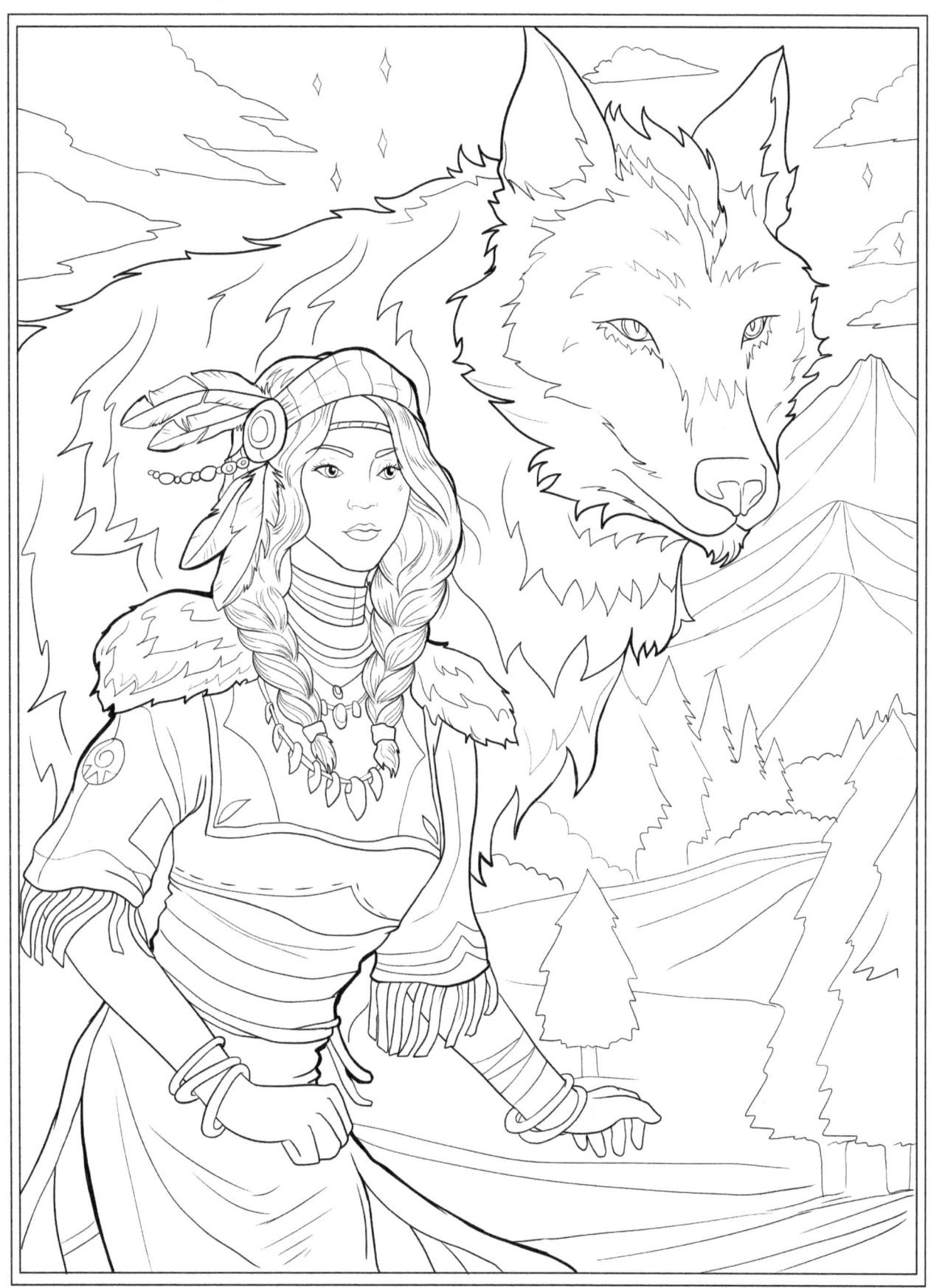

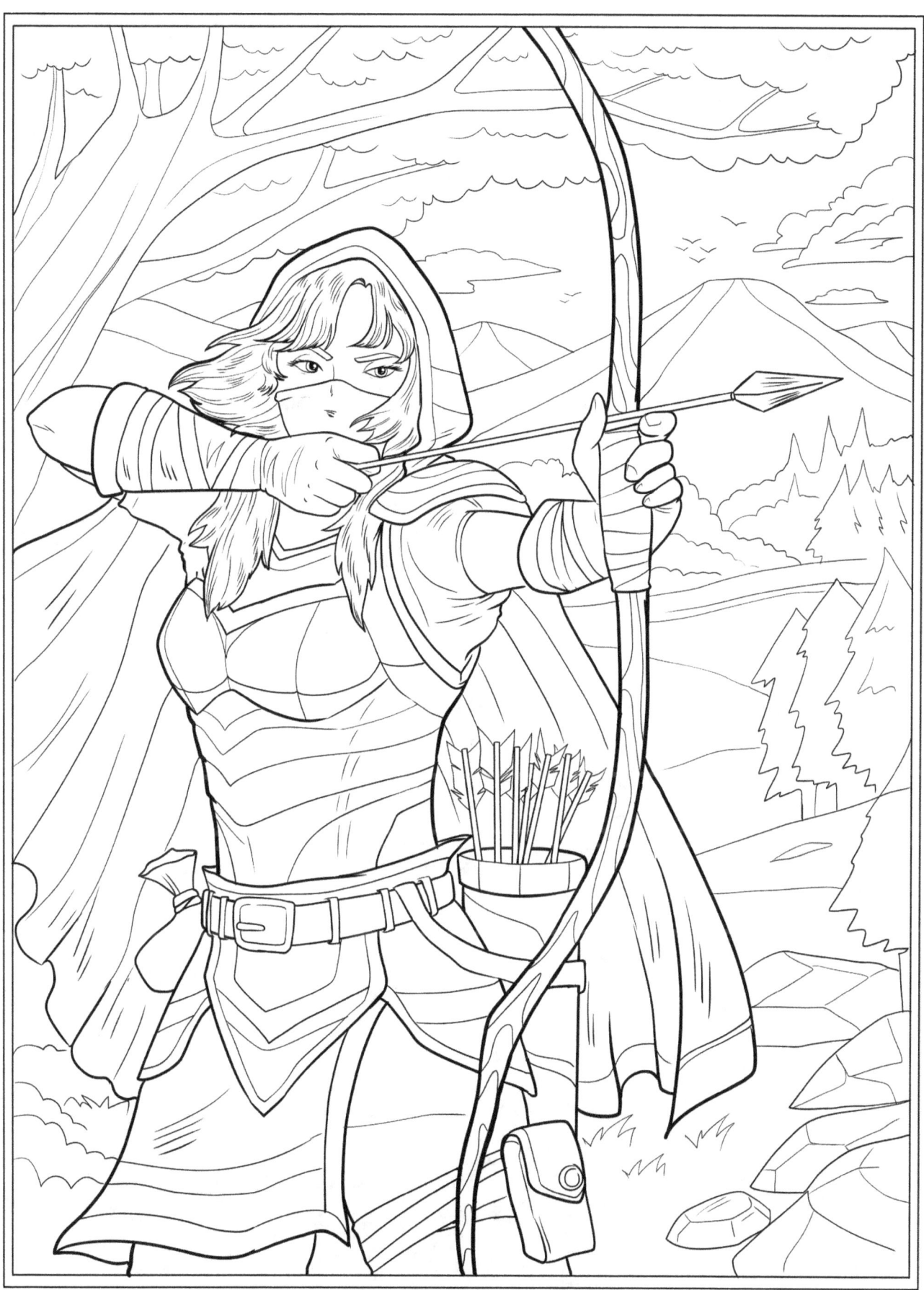

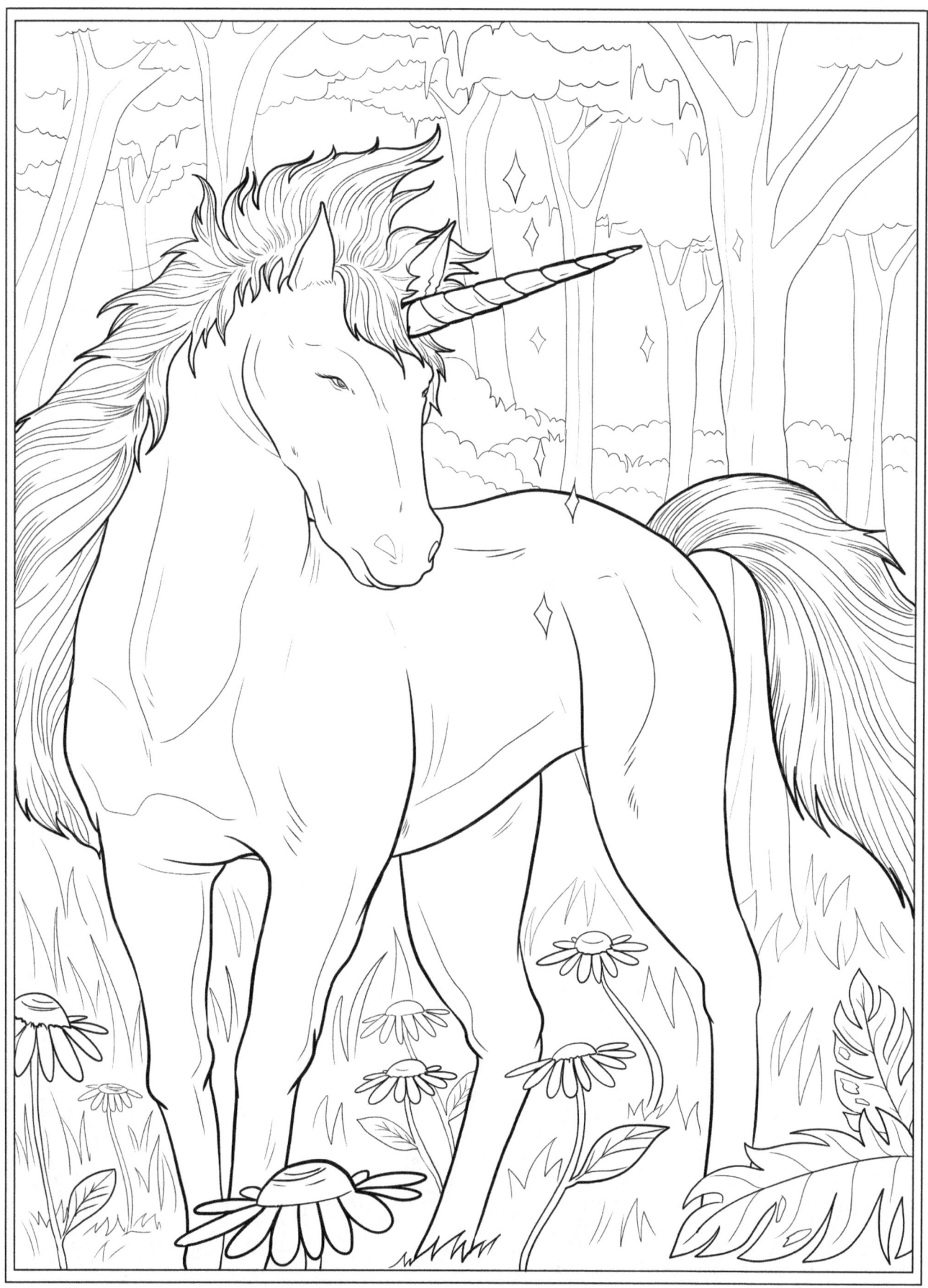

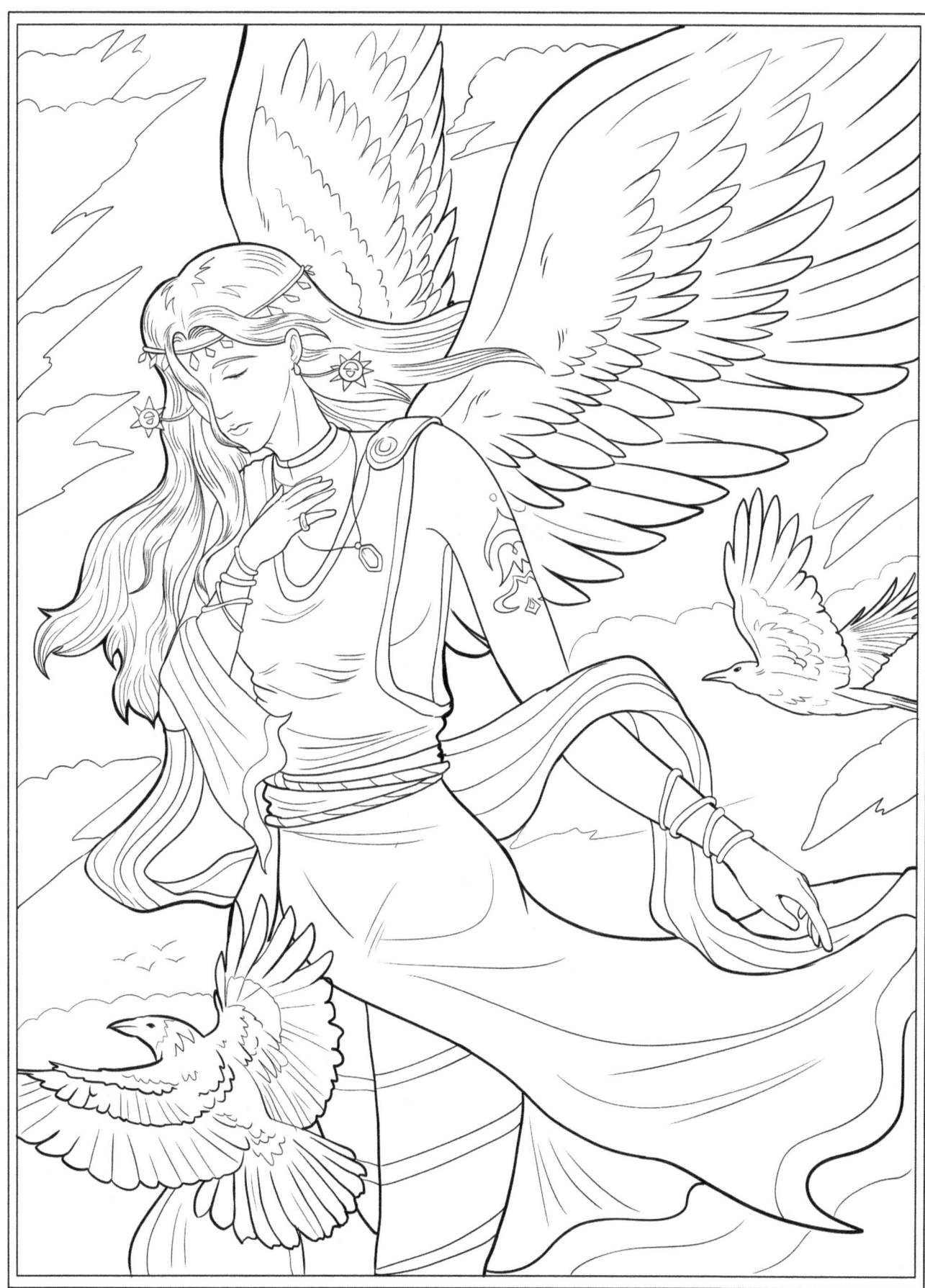

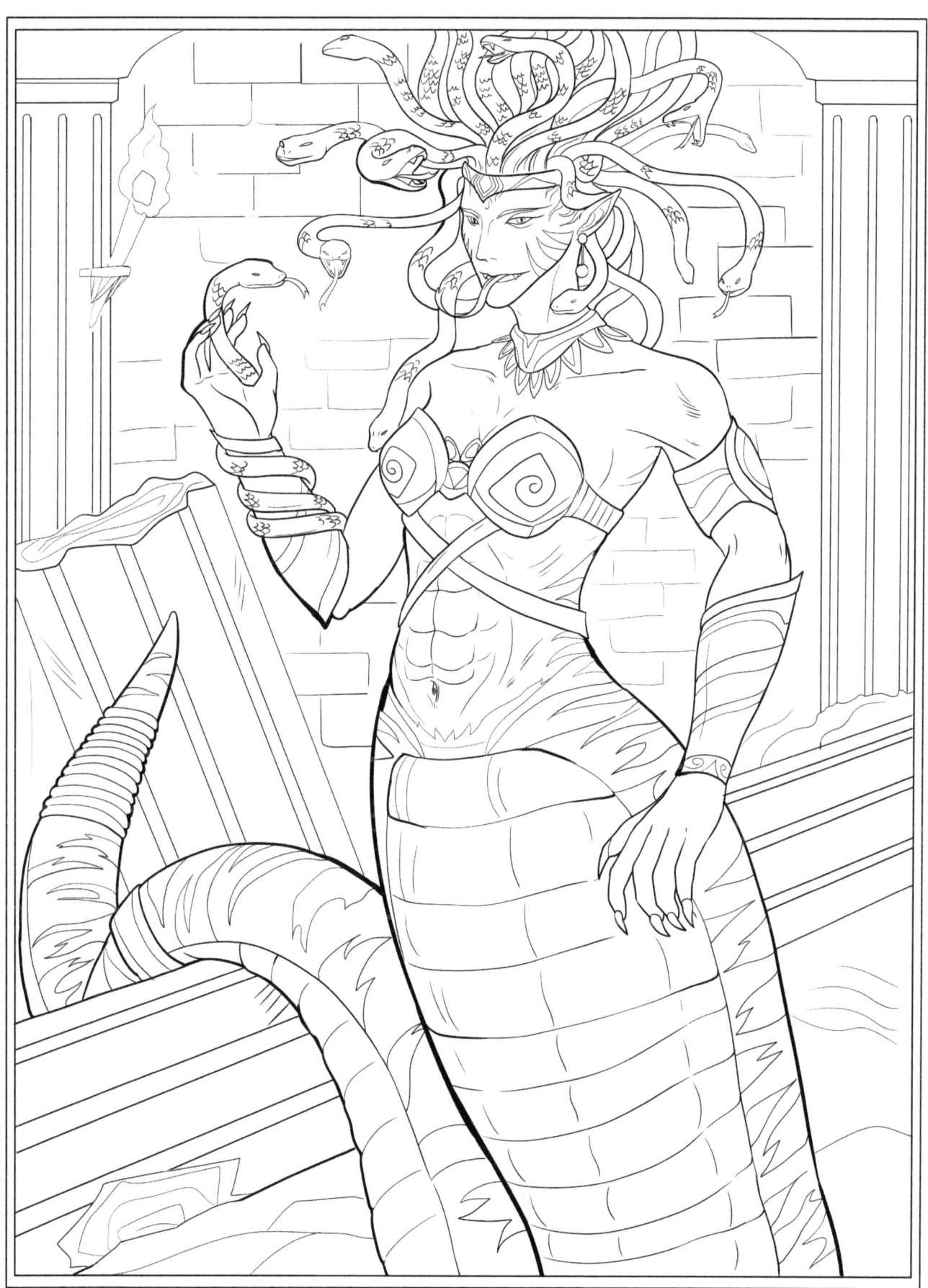

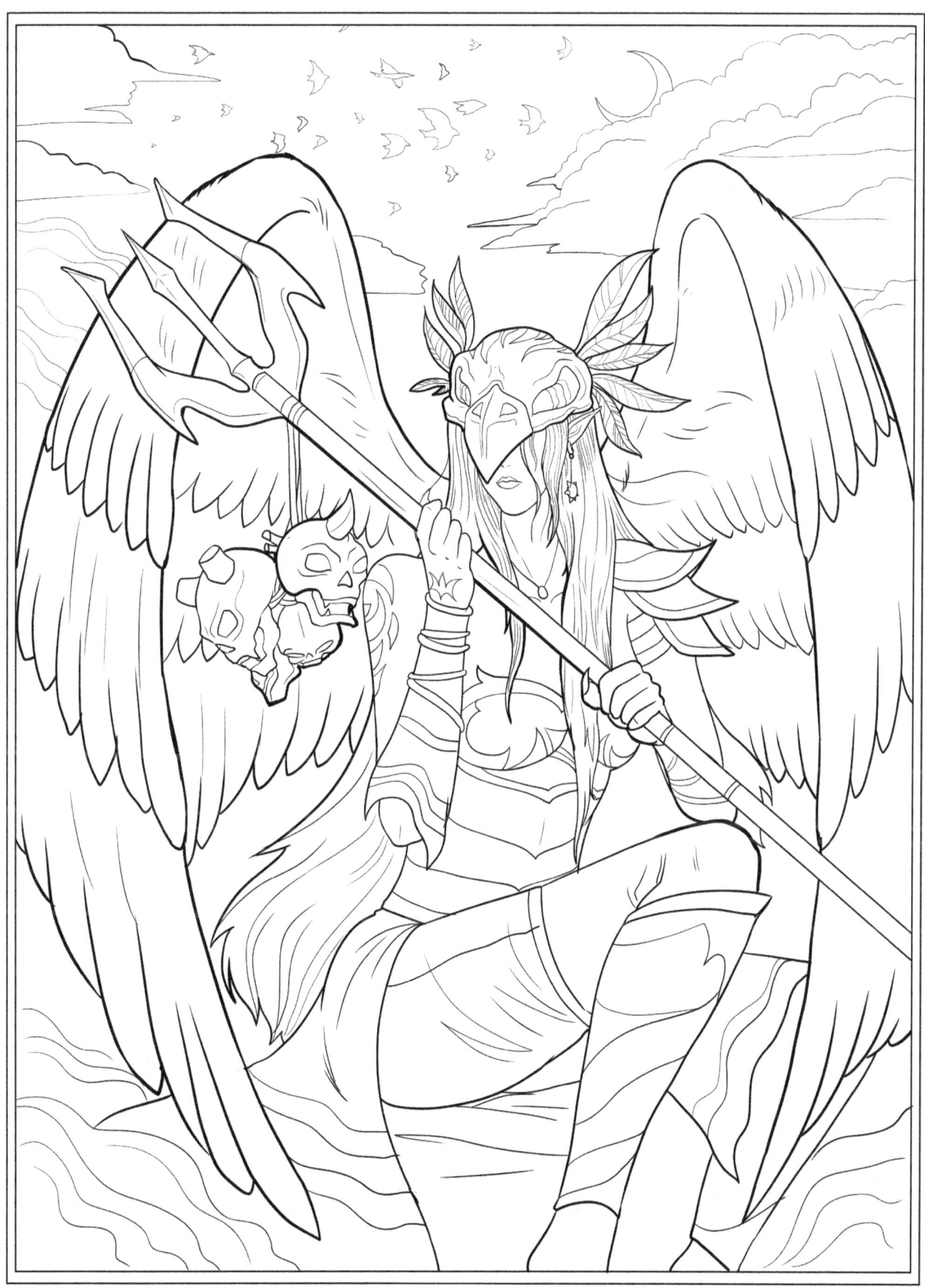

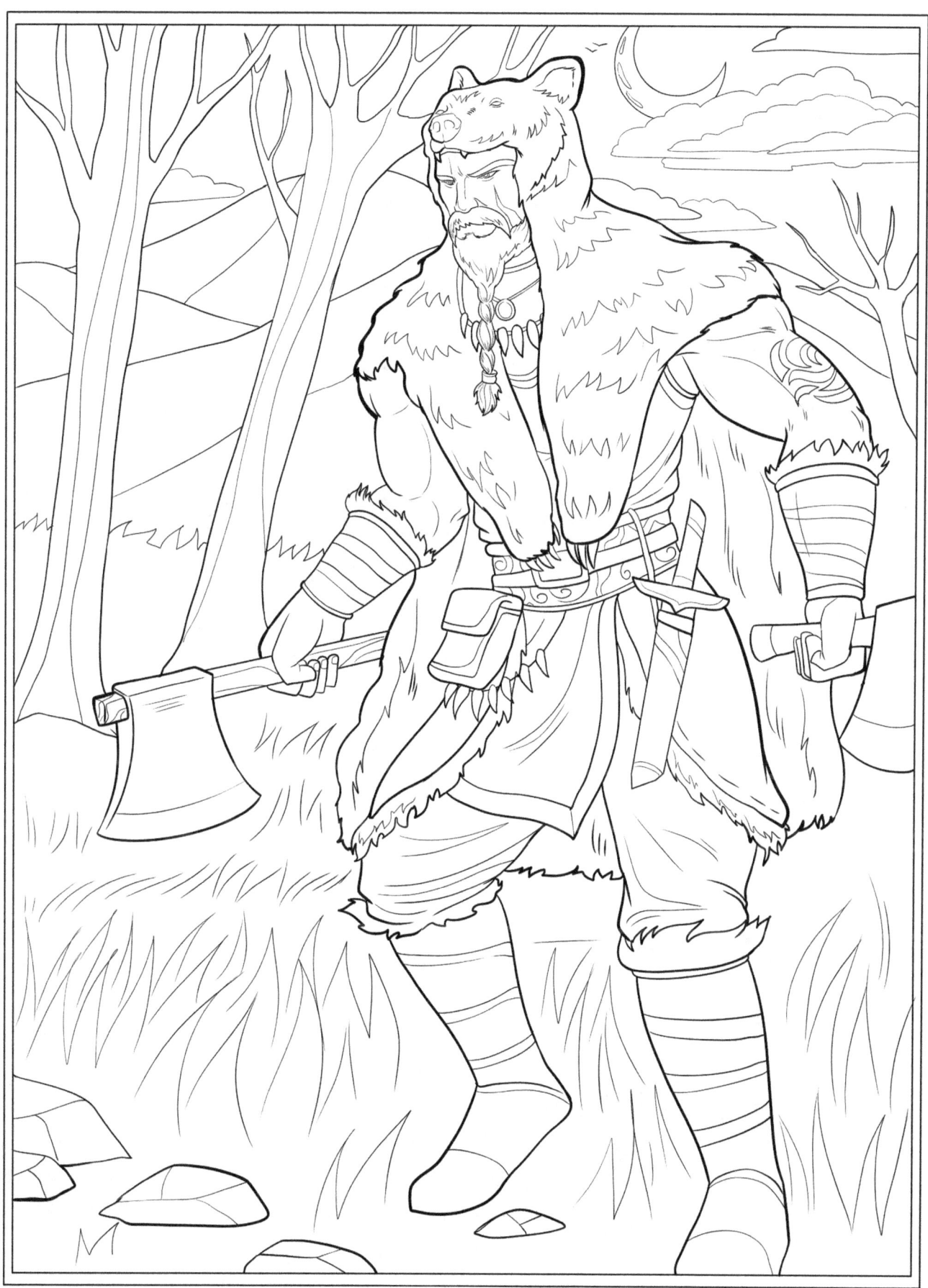

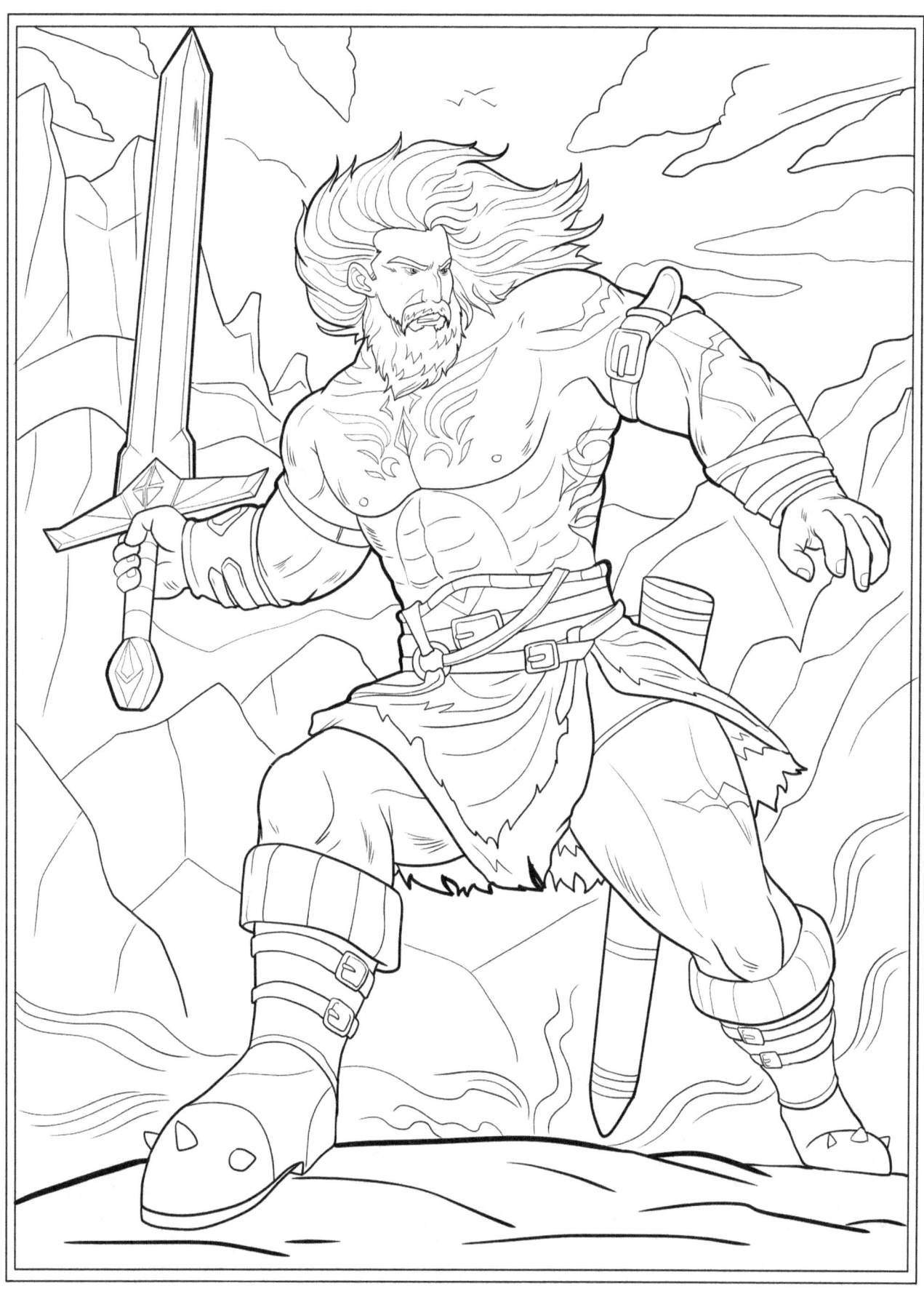

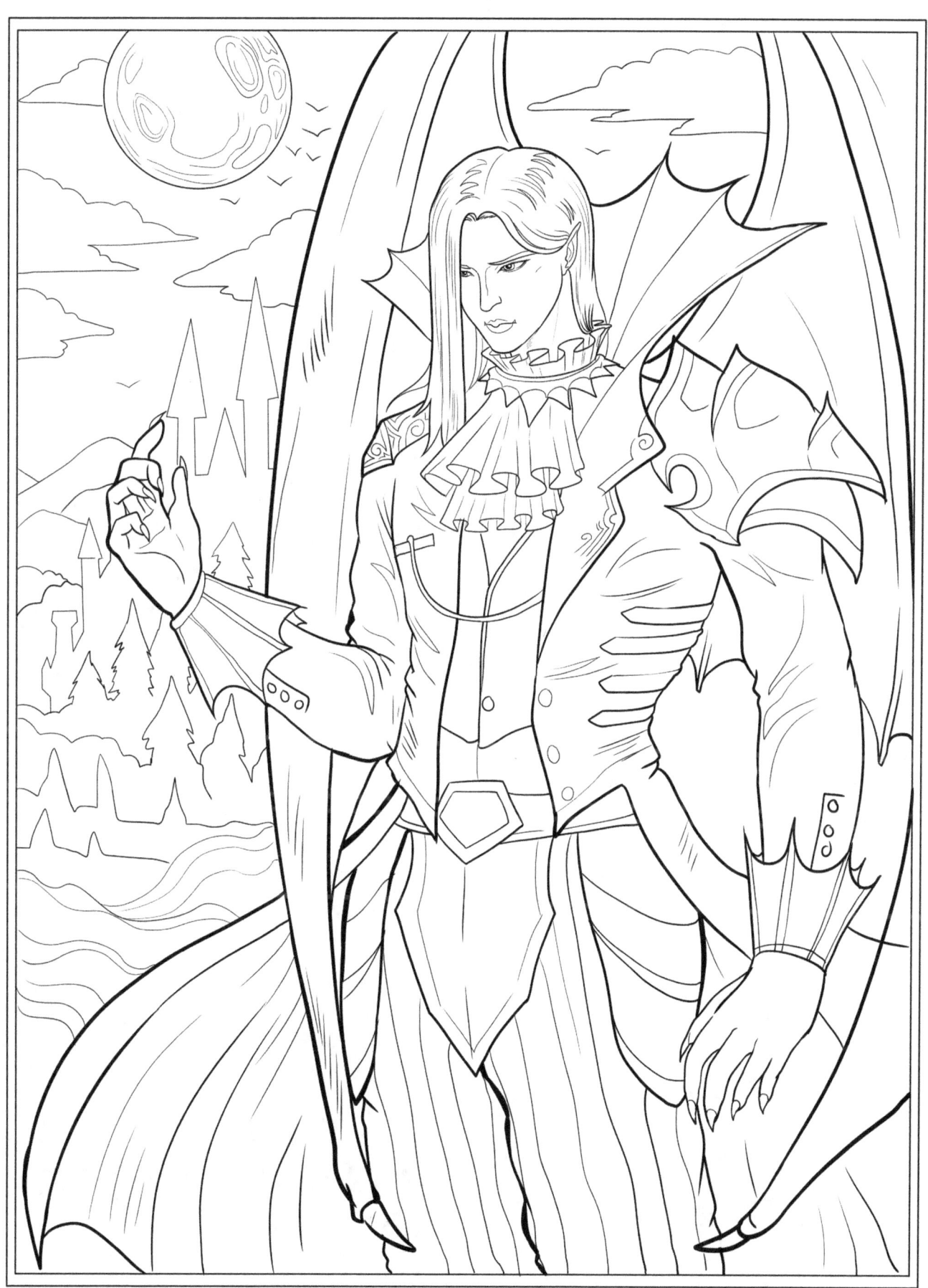

www.ingramcontent.com/pod-product-compliance
Lightning Source LLC
Chambersburg PA
CBHW081452220526
45466CB00008B/2605